CW01621470

# WARRIOR SLAY

## *Win in Worship and Slay When You Pray*

*31 Day Devotional Journey to Healing and Breakthrough*

*Patrice Burrell*

# Copyright

Warrior Slay: Win in Worship and Slay When you Pray



www.patriceburrell.com



Editing by: Armor of Hope Writing and Publishing Services, LLC

Printed in the United States of America

ISBN: 978-0-692-10799-7

First Edition

# Warrior Slay

## *Win in Worship and Slay When You Pray*

# Dedication

For my warrior princess,

*Jalauria*

May the worshiper within always rise to slay.

You were created by God to win.

# Table of Contents

# ~DAY 1~
# GOD HEARS YOUR CRY

Scripture Reading: Psalm 30:2

Ask any mother of a newborn baby, and she will tell you that nothing quite compares to or stirs the soul as does the sound of hearing your sweet bundle of joy cry out helplessly. The sound of a baby's cry can communicate a myriad of things to the ear of an attentive mother. Maybe it is a cry that longs for the tender affection that can only be satisfied when cradled in Mommy's arms. Maybe it is a cry that signals attention needed because of hunger or a soiled diaper that needs changing. Perhaps it is a cry of distress that undoubtedly leads the mother to believe her baby is in physical discomfort. It has been said that the closest love on earth a human being can receive, that even gives an inkling of an idea of God's agape love for us, is experienced in the love a mother expresses to her child.

God is not only our creator, but He is our Father. His tender, father-heart towards us far exceeds our best effort to imagine how much He loves us. Just like a mother hears the cry of her baby, God hears us each time we cry out to Him. Not only does He see every tear we cry, but He hears our silent cry that has no voice. He sees deeply into who we really are, way past our outward appearance. He hears and sees the cry of our heart. The good news is, He is faithful to respond to our cry, no matter how faint it may be or how depleted we may feel.

As you begin day one of this devotional journey, there are a few things you need to resolve within yourself. First, settle within yourself that even as you are believing God to heal and manifest breakthrough in areas of your life, you must know that the reason you find yourself in need of such a healing and breakthrough has nothing to do with God not loving you. God desires that you be healed and receive breakthrough more than you have the capacity to desire it for yourself. You cannot do, un-do, or not do, anything that would cause the Father to stop loving you relentlessly. No matter how you may feel, the truth is, there is nothing about you that can ever cause his love for you to diminish. The greatest lies the enemy will always try to make you wrestle with about yourself are: "I'm not loveable, I'm not worthy, and I'm not good enough." God is concerned about everything that concerns you. He wants to heal you and make you whole in every area of your life, from the inside out.

Secondly, settle within yourself that believing God is worth the faith and hope you expend in this process. Believing is not only the confession of your belief, but it is also the activation and release of your faith. It is more than what we say with words from our lips; it's the attitude of our heart. Both must be in agreement with the Spirit of God that leads us into all truth and freedom in Him.

Finally, settle within yourself that God is able and He will come through for you. Be fully convinced that nothing is impossible if you believe in God. May your courage dispel your doubts. God is the only one who sees and hears every tear that falls from your eyes and lovingly bottles them to pour back upon you unimaginable blessings (Psalm 56:8, NLT). As a good, loving father, He wants to heal you completely. He wants you to experience breakthrough personally, relationally, financially, emotionally, mentally, and physically.

When every area of your life is in balance according to the will of God, not only can you be healed, but you can be made whole. Wholeness is necessary in order to experience sustained victory that has already been accessed for you by Jesus. So go ahead and cry, let it all out. Be brave enough to believe. God is your healer, and He is right in your midst to hear your cry and heal every place within you.

<u>Scripture Reference:</u> Psalm 30:2 (NKJV)

O Lord my God, I cried out to you, and you healed me.

Prayer Points: personal reflection, repentance, and renewal

In My Own Words: (Construct Your Personalized Prayer):

Faith Declaration: Thank you Lord that you hear me, help me, and heal me every time I cry out to you.

Journal Activity: Reflect upon the areas of your life that are in need of healing and breakthrough. Consider relationships and circumstances you are presently dealing with, not limiting yourself to only physical wellness within your body. What are some of the obstacles facing you from receiving breakthrough? Is there anything specifically you need to bring before God in a spirit of repentance? How is God drawing you to experience renewal in your relationship with Him?

Journaling Notes:

Prayer Confession Day 1: A Prayer for Restoration

Heavenly Father, I begin this devotional journey today by giving you praise. I confess that you are good, gracious, worthy, and wise. Thank You for this opportunity to come into your presence with a heart, mind, and mouth filled with your praise.

I come to you transparent, withholding nothing, spiritually naked and vulnerable. I recognize that you are the one and only person I can be completely broken before. Yet, you will not reject me. As your daughter, I acknowledge that I need you desperately. The thought of doing life without you or even on my own terms is completely meaningless. I am eternally grateful that you made a way for me to experience your love through Jesus. I am so glad I can have my own relationship with you.

Today, I ask you to restore me. Every place within me that needs your touch, I pray that you would breathe on me. Even right now, I repent of my sin, and I ask you to cleanse me. Give me a heart and mind that wants to obey your Word and surrender to your plan for my life. Help me to submit even in the areas I have struggled to relinquish control. I realize this is necessary so that I can be made whole in you.

Holy Spirit, restore my joy, my strength, and my will to be the woman you have called me to be. Restore my spirit that has been worn and weary from the cares of this world. Where I have been crushed by frustration, distracted by disappointments, and overwhelmed by my own inadequacies – where I have believed lies from the enemy and proven negligent in my ability to recover on my own - today I cry out to you, Lord! Help me! Father, restore my soul. Lead me in paths of righteousness for your name's sake. Guide me into refreshing green pastures. Instead of being overtaken by rushing waters that would overwhelm my soul, allow me to drink from them calmly. Help me to remember that you are my living well and the only source that will never run dry. In Jesus' name, I pray, amen.

# ~DAY 2~
# SAVE ME, RESCUE ME

Scripture Reading: Jeremiah 17:14

In some way, shape, or form, most of us have been confronted with sickness in our body. Not all sickness we encounter throughout the course of life is terminal. However, that does not mean that living with symptoms and a diagnosis is not accompanied by its fair share of challenges. Many people exhaust their time, energy, and resources trying to manage pain. I am reminded of the woman described in the Bible as having an "issue of blood." In Mark 5:25-34 (see verse 26), it explains that she spent all she had trying to get a breakthrough in her physical health. It wasn't until she pressed her way through a crowd of people to touch Jesus that she was made whole.

Healing and wholeness are strongly connected, yet there is a slight distinction. The word "heal" comes from the Greek word ***iaomai***, meaning "to cure" (Strong's G2390). The word "whole" is translated from the Greek word ***sozo***, meaning "to save" (Strong's G4982). Like the woman with the issue of blood, we should not only want to be healed from disease. We should also desire to be saved and delivered from the destruction and suffering disease often inflicts. This can cause one to perish - spirit, body, and soul. The same way we need our spirit to be saved or rescued is the same way our body and soul needs to be made whole.

Jesus wants to save us from hurt and damaged emotions. He wants to rescue us from the cycles of torment and anguish that replay in our minds. What good is it to be healed on the outside but not be whole within? This is why we must be healed from the inside out. It is one thing to battle sickness in our body, but it is another to be afflicted in our minds and emotions.

When you have been rescued and saved by God, praise naturally follows. As a matter of fact, it is the overflow of your gratitude. When you have been in bondage to anything-sickness, sin, and sometimes even yourself, to be rescued by God is to experience breakthrough and great freedom. But being able to praise God even when you are in the midst of dealing with sickness, pain, diagnosis, and symptoms require an unwavering commitment to faith. It takes faith to realize that God deserves our praise just because he is always there wanting to heal and rescue us. It takes faith to believe that the manifestation we so desperately desire will come to pass. This type of conviction will cause us to praise him in advance.

Will you accept my challenge today to praise Him right now? I realize that you may be in a hard place if you are suffering in your health, mind, or emotions. However, I need to also remind you, my sister warrior, praise is the starting point to worship and prayer. You can win in worship, and you will slay every obstacle when you pray. To get there, first you must begin with a praise that acknowledges that God is trustworthy, and He is sovereignly in absolute control of it all. This praise resolves your assured emergence as the victor – even if you don't see it right this moment. God is faithful. He knows. He cares. He sees. He rescues. Just hold on. He is strengthening you to wait in Him. It's coming to pass.

<u>Scripture Reference:</u> Jeremiah 17:14 (NKJV)

Heal me, O Lord, and I shall be healed; save me, and I shall be saved, for you are my praise.

<u>Prayer Points:</u> Keep your eyes on God; do not allow distractions to pull you away from the presence of God. Enlarge God in your heart and mind-not your challenges. Spend time in worship so that as you

give God your attention, His presence causes every concern to dissipate.

In My Own Words: (Construct Your Personalized Prayer):

Faith Declaration: I praise you because you are mighty to save and make me whole. I confess you as my healer and deliverer.

Journal Activity: Identify the specific healing you are believing God for by journaling a prayer of praise directly to God. Don't be intimidated or afraid to call out by name exactly what you are believing God to manifest. Remember to seal your prayer with praise.

Journaling Notes:

Prayer Confession Day 2: A Prayer for Focus

Father, today I choose to praise you on purpose! I will not be moved by people around me, my circumstances, or even my own feelings. Despite the challenges I face in my body, in my relationships, in my finances, in my emotions, and in my mind, I still choose to submit myself completely to you. I decree by my own words my commitment, nevertheless, to remain focused on you! I know that you hear me and save me every time I cry out to you. Rescue me from any sickness in my body, illness in my thoughts, and ailments in my emotions. I confess that you are my God and my healer.

I believe your word in 2 Thessalonians 3:3 (NIV) that says, "The Lord is faithful, and he will strengthen and protect you from the evil one." Lord, no matter what the enemy may attempt to do to break my focus, I trust you to protect and guard me from every attack. I declare that my eyes are fixed upon you. I will not be moved by distractions. I declare that I stand strong in faith because I stand strong in you, holding fast to your Word that cannot return unto you void.

I can praise you for unshakable, unstoppable, and unsinkable, faith despite tests and trials that confront me. I will not be afraid! When the storm blows over, I will still be standing in you. I choose to rest in you as an act of my faith and obedience to your Word. Yes, I believe that I will live to see the goodness of the Lord in the land of the living as I daily live in your presence. In Jesus 'name, I pray, amen.

# ~DAY 3~
# He Lives In Me

Scripture Reading: Romans 8:11

Have you ever really stopped to consider how much power you have? I realize you may not necessarily feel powerful at this exact moment. In fact, you may have laughed inwardly to yourself, kind of the way Sarah did when God told her she would have a baby way past her childbearing years. Or, maybe you quickly dismissed the thought because no matter how much you try to convince yourself, you just can't seem to wrap your brain around the notion that *you* actually possess the same power as Jesus. Possibly, you know you have the capacity to display that power. Maybe in your head, you've come to terms with your ability to do so. Yet, from time to time, you still struggle in your heart. This can make it difficult to maintain consistency in operating in your God-given power.

Now, consider this, have you ever really stopped to evaluate how much power your omnipotent God contains? Well, He is limitless, unrestricted, and abounding in power beyond our human ability to comprehend. And because of this, we have unlimited potential and limitless resources since His same Spirit lives in us. I don't know about you, but I need His power to be active and living in me! How ineffective life would be to have access to a power source, yet never choose to tap into it and be charged.

When we just stop and think about what power it took to raise Jesus from the dead, the very act in and of itself is amazing. What's even more amazing is how the same power is still available to give us life in our very human existence. What sickness, disease, or illness can be bigger than that power? What heaviness, burden, or care of this life? The answer is none! There is nothing more powerful than the power of God.

As kingdom citizens, when we understand how this power works, we also begin to understand how we can exercise our authority. God's power activated in us equals authority! Do not be afraid to exercise your power and authority when it comes to standing in faith to believe God's promises for you.

You have every right to expect the manifestations of healing and breakthrough. You have every right to confess what you are believing based upon the Word of God. You have every right to reject any and every action not aligned with the will of God concerning you. Use the power that God has given you to boldly declare your authority. Remember, it is not in your strength or in your own authority, but it is in the same power that raised Jesus from the dead that's alive and active within you!

<u>Scripture Reference:</u> Romans 8:11 (NKJV)

But if the Spirit of Him who raised Jesus from the dead dwells in you, He who raised Christ from the dead will also give life to your mortal bodies through His Spirit who dwells in you.

<u>Prayer Points:</u> Every physical ailment-terminal illness, chronic illness, occasional sickness-they are all subject to the authority of the word of God. Speak the Word of God over pain and symptoms; plead the blood of Jesus over your physical body.

<u>In My Own Words: (Construct Your Personalized Prayer):</u>

______________________________________________________

______________________________________________________

______________________________________________________

Faith Declaration: Thank you, Father, that your spirit dwells in me and quickens my mortal body that I may live the abundant life you died for me to experience.

Journal Activity: Make a list of everything you desire God's spirit to empower you to accomplish physically. Maybe you are presently unable to engage in some of these activities, but how do you see your current condition changing by the power of God? What is God asking you to do in this process?

Journaling Notes:

Prayer Confession Day 3: A Prayer for Healing

Lord, thank you for being my healer. I refuse to believe, accept, or confess anything else over my life. I believe in the power of speaking your Word over myself. I know you have given me this power to exercise great faith! Thank you that no situation is too difficult for you, and despite what I may feel, even in my body, I know that you are working in my circumstances. Manifestation of breakthrough and healing is mine!

I am grateful for medical expertise that you have provided to me. I am also grateful that you have educated me to understand the difference between facts and truth. Regardless of what the facts may be, the truth of the matter is by the stripes of Jesus, I am already healed! According to Isaiah 53:5 (NKJV): "Jesus was wounded for our transgressions, He was bruised for our iniquities; the chastisement for our peace was upon Him, and by His stripes we are healed." Jesus is my great physician, hallelujah!

I confess that I am healed from all minor sickness and life-threatening disease that would attempt to afflict my body. Every physical ailment, terminal illness, chronic symptom, and occasional sickness is subject to the authority of the blood of Jesus. Pain is not my portion! I receive the relief of God that comes from your healing virtue to permeate and penetrate every place where I hurt.

My body is healed and whole. It shall function as it has been designed to function. There is nothing missing or lacking in my health. My body is the temple of the Holy Spirit, and it will be in perfect alignment that God may be glorified in me. I declare my healing, and it's in Jesus' name, I pray, amen.

# ~DAY 4~

# Remember All That He's Already Done

Scripture Reading: Psalm 103:1-5

Memory is a unique ability God has gifted each of us with. Although we may not always view it as a gift, and not every memory is one we care to be reminded of, sometimes it is necessary to take a moment, pause and look back over our lives and consider how faithful our God has been. Memory is a powerful tool we can readily access when we simply take the time to sit and reflect on how far we have come because of God's grace.

James admonished the early church to count it all joy whenever you are faced with various trials (James 1:2 RSV). What if we took that verse literally? I believe that at every turn, through it all - the good, bad, crazy, sad-we can still trace the hand of God at work on our behalf. There were and still are blessings to count in the midst of being in what may feel like a very hard place.

I love how the psalmist declares with great conviction his decision to remain in a posture of praise at all times (see Psalm 103:1-5)! As he takes inventory of all the Lord has done, without reservation, he can boldly exclaim an attitude of praise. When you are in the eye of the storm, it sometimes becomes difficult to bless God while confronted with adversity. If we are honest, the weight of our burden can feel so unbearable that finding a "right-now" praise seems unattainable. However, if we can manage to remember…and allow the memories of God's benefits and blessings to console us, comfort us, and convince us, we too will join with the psalmist to proclaim God's praise in the midst of whatever we presently may be confronting.

Particularly when you are believing for healing in your body, it can be very easy to focus on the pain. In my own experience, there was a season in my life when I felt consumed with trying to manage my pain. In my questioning to God about why I had to endure such a level of intense physical suffering, he lovingly replied, "I wanted to see how you would respond to me at your greatest point of pain." In that moment, I knew exactly what He meant. My Father wanted to see if Judah would come forth; if the warrior down on the inside would allow praise to arise.

The reality of the situation is, no matter how badly we may feel, just as loving and forgiving is a choice, so is praising. I challenge you today to praise God on purpose, even in the midst of pain and heartache; even in the middle of your test and trial. Take this moment to step away from where you are now and recall the goodness, the faithfulness of everything God has already done for you. Stir your memory to recount how God has delivered you in times past by His strong arm. And even though it may be hard for you to see right now, in the eye of your storm, He is there with you, as He's always been.

Do you remember the three Hebrew boys in their fire blazing pit? Do you recall Daniel in the den of lions? Do you remember Joseph in prison and David when he faced Goliath? Most of all, do you remember your own history with God? Don't ever forget how honorable His reputation is with you. Since he's delivered you before, you can rest confidently in knowing He will do it again. Sometimes we just need to stop and remember. He's still upholding you, and He promises to never leave you or forsake you. Why don't you begin to celebrate and give Him praise now?

Scripture Reference: Psalm 103:1-5 (NKJV)

Bless the Lord, O my soul; And all that is within me, bless His holy name! Bless the Lord, O my soul, and forget not all His benefits: who forgives all your iniquities, who heals all your diseases, who redeems your life from destruction, who crowns you with lovingkindness and tender mercies, who satisfies your mouth with good things, so that your youth is renewed like the eagle's.

Prayer Points: faith to believe again and hope to be restored; confidence to align our words with the word of God; receive wholeness mentally and emotionally that works in unity with physical manifestations of healing

In My Own Words: (Construct Your Personalized Prayer):

Faith Declaration: I will bless the Lord, not only because he is my healer, but also because He forgives me of my iniquities and is my redeemer. Thank you for your tender Father-heart that always satisfies me with good things because of your unfailing love and mercies.

Journal Activity: Recount everything that has already happened in your life where it seemed like a bad situation, but God brought forth beauty and blessings.

Journaling Notes:

Prayer Confession Day 4: A Prayer of Reassurance

Father, as I reflect and remember, I can praise you for your faithfulness to me. There has never been a time in my life you were not with me. Thank you for reminding me of your steadfast love for me. I have no doubt that you are moving in my midst today and working through my situation for my good. You are a good Father with good gifts and plans for me. I won't be moved by what I encounter in the natural because it is temporary and subject to change at any moment.

Today, I confess that your track record and credit are perfect. I am securely reassured that as I continue to worship and pray; I am that much closer to receiving the healing and breakthrough you have already freely given me. I declare manifestation is on the way! Just because I may not have it at this moment does not mean it will not suddenly show up. I expect to see your glory on display on my behalf. As I wait in you, I access memories of what you've already done for me, and how time after time, you've proven yourself to me. This is why I can rejoice! This is why I can remain hopeful and full of faith! This is why I choose to praise you. I command the warrior on the inside of me to arise! In Jesus' name, I pray, amen.

# ~DAY 5~
# STRONGER THAN YOU THINK

Scripture Reading: Isaiah 40:29

Can I tell you a secret? You are the opposite of everything the devil has ever told you about yourself. As a matter of fact, anything he tells you is a lie, because he is the father of lies. On the contrary, God does not even have the ability to lie since it is not in His nature. Therefore, everything He has ever spoken to you is true and worthy of your complete trust. Truth is rooted and grounded in the Word of God. We should always be professing His Word from our lips.

There are three things we must constantly guard: our heart, our mind, and our mouth. Each of these areas must be filled with confessions of what God has already established about our identity in Him. This takes faith on our part! Is that what it means to walk by faith? If we only confessed what we could see or what we feel, we would never receive the fullness of God in our lives. Things are never truly as they seem, so don't be moved by what you see. As for feelings, they can be likened to a roller coaster ride - up one moment and down the next. This is why we must know the Word of God and know it for ourselves. Knowing what God says eliminates our tendency to error based upon what we see or feel.

You are stronger than you think. No, really! You have incredible stamina - mentally, emotionally, and yes, physically. Even when you think or feel that you are weak, Isaiah reminds us that our God gives power to the weak and increases our strength (Isaiah 40:29).

Who can argue with that? If God is lifting you up in His strength, never allow anyone to make you feel inferior (not even you).

Today, I encourage you to persevere in your faith, and by faith, confess that you are strong enough to make it to the other side (the other side is better known as victory)! May the Spirit of Might come upon you like never before and may your trust and confidence in Him be unshakable. You are who God says you are, and He says you are well able to emerge from this challenge with great victory because in your weakness, His strength is made perfect. You ARE stronger than you think!

Scripture Reference: Isaiah 40:29 (NKJV)

He gives power to the weak, and to those who have no might, He increases strength.

Prayer Points: the spirit of might to be upon you; the ability to persevere in faith; the ability to trust God and rest in Him

In My Own Words: (Construct Your Personalized Prayer):

Faith Declaration: Father, even when I feel weak, I will say that I am strong, because your power gives me strength.

Journal Activity: As awkward as this may feel, create a list of all of your positive characteristics, talents, and abilities. What are you good at or strong in? Do you realize God's grace is the power at work enabling you to be the wonderful person you are and do all of the wonderful things you can? Give yourself a break! And give yourself permission to be grateful for all of the ways you show forth His strength.

Journaling Notes:

Prayer Confession Day 5: A Prayer for Renewed Strength

Father, thank you for reminding me today that I am stronger than I have realized. I am still here in the land of the living to call out to you. That means you are sustaining and maintaining me, despite what I may see in the natural or how I may even feel or think. I confess today that your strength is lifting me above anything that would seek to hold me down. For this, Father, I can offer you praise!

I declare out of my own mouth that I will persevere in faith by your grace. I refuse to give up, and I will not quit. I am anointed to finish strong and stand fast in the confession of my faith. Everything you have promised me shall come to pass. When I feel like I am about to faint, fall, or falter, your strength will refresh me. I will wait patiently for your perfect timing to manifest the deliverance, healing, and breakthrough you've already given me. It must materialize because you have declared it to be so according to your Word.

Thank you for your power that causes me to trust you and rest in you today. Thank you for your power that causes me to keep going. Thank you for your power to speak the right words in my circumstance or even a negative situation. Thank you for your mighty power that reminds me you are a mighty God. I am strong in you, and I receive renewed strength this day. In Jesus' mighty name I pray, amen.

# ~DAY 6~
# STAY IN THE WORD

Scripture Reading: Psalm 107:20

How profound a statement to reveal the magnitude of God's Word: "*For assuredly, I say to you, till heaven and earth pass away, one jot or one tittle will by no means pass from the law till all is fulfilled*" (Matthew 5:18 NKJV ). The foundation of our Christian walk with God must be established in and sustained by the Word of God. Yet, how many people can honestly say spending time in the Word of God is consistently the priority of their day? That means we order our day around the Word - not do everything else first and then try to squeeze our Bible study, reading, or devotional times with God afterward.

Interestingly enough, Jesus understood an important principle that all too many born-again believers have not grasped. In Luke 4:1-13, we see that each time the devil reared his ugly face to challenge our Savior with temptation in the wilderness, Jesus defeated Him by speaking the Word of God. In order to overcome the enemy, you must use the Word of God like a sword (Ephesians 6:17). Sometimes, the problem to solve is this, "What if you're not familiar enough with the Word to properly execute it when in battle? The answer is sadly obvious. You will probably succumb to feelings of defeat even though Jesus has already made provision for you to experience victory.

In Psalm 119:11, we learn that God's Word should be hidden in our heart. If something is in your heart, it is always with you because it is a part of you. It is the job of all believers to become students of the Word of God. This is not just reserved for clergy, seminarians, or theologians, but it is our right and responsibility as Children of God to write God's word upon the tablet of our heart. The scripture reference for today declares that God sent his word to heal and deliver from destruction (Psalm 107:20). This is another reminder of how powerful the Word of God is. It also reveals authority in speaking the Word of God. This same power and authority is yours for the taking.

Being with God daily in His Word helps us to fortify ourselves against the attack of the enemy. If we "store up our timber" (as the old folks would say), then when in battle we will be ready to release the Word of God against the attack of the enemy. But remember, you've got to have something to draw from. Practice the presence of God by speaking aloud his Word. Study to show yourself approved unto God (2 Timothy 2:15). His word is your weapon! It is sharper than any other device (Hebrews 4:12). Meditate on God's word day and night so that you may be as stable as a tree planted by a river of water, with roots richly nurtured from being in the presence of God (Psalm 1). We stay in the word daily so that our lives will stay connected to the heart of our Father. He is our power source; He is our deliverer. He is the Word of God!

Scripture Reference: Psalm 107:20 (KJV)

He sent his word, and healed them, and delivered them from their destructions.

Prayer Points: Have eyes to see God as your personal deliverer; confess Him as being exalted above everything you are challenged with in the natural. Declare the authority and power of the Word.

In My Own Words: (Construct Your Personalized Prayer):

____________________________________________________________

____________________________________________________________

____________________________________________________________

____________________________________________________________

____________________________________________________________

Faith Declaration: Thank you Father for sending your word that I may be healed. Today, I firmly stand on the Word of God and declare that you have delivered me from all destruction, hallelujah!

Journal Activity: What's foremost on your prayer list? Research scriptures for every situation you are currently facing. Ask the Holy Spirit to guide you as you look to match the correct scriptures. Find God's promises to you through His word and pray these scriptures during your prayer time. You may even find it helpful to carry a pocket size journal, index cards, or sticky notes with these scriptures recorded. Every time you physically eat a meal, take a moment to "eat" spiritually the Word of God by speaking aloud one or two of your scriptures.

Journaling Notes:

Prayer Confession Day 6: A Prayer for Living in the Word

Lord, I praise you for your Word! I renew my commitment to live in your Word consistently. I ask that you would help me to cherish being with you above all else. Whatever stops me from fully receiving your Word, please remove it from me. Do not allow anything to distract me from spending time each day reading, meditating, or studying your Word. Help me to value it in such a way that reading the Bible is a high priority in my lifestyle. I resolve to make time to be in the Word because the Word of God is foundational to my spiritual growth.

I confess that I am deeply anchored in your Word. In the face of difficulty, I cannot be moved because your Word is hidden in my heart. I am destined to emerge victorious and triumphant because of the authority of your Word. Psalm 119:130 (NLT) declares, "The teaching of your Word gives light, so even the simple can understand." There is no issue in my life that your Word cannot handle. I thank you for the power, direction, and clarity that comes with your Word. I boldly proclaim your Word over my life this day. It will have the final authority over all that governs my actions and reactions. I will not be moved or shaken because your Word makes me secure.

Thank you, Father, for sending your Word to heal me and make me whole in every aspect of my life. Thank you that your Word ministers deliverance to my soul. There is no destruction that can befall me that is greater than your Word! Your Word is true because you are true. I firmly stand with assurance upon your Word, active and alive in me! In Jesus's name I pray, amen.

# ~DAY 7~
# How Much More?

Scripture Reading: Psalm 34:19

How much more? Now there's a question (rest assured) we have all asked God at some point along the way. How much more can I take of this…how much more can I bear…how much longer before breakthrough? Sometimes it seems like everything is happening all at once and the end is nowhere in sight. A friend of mine once told me that strong Christians often have multiple darts thrown at them. Why? The enemy understands that to release one at a time would be ineffective for a spiritually mature Christian. In this light, we should consider ourselves blessed that God counts us worthy to be tested. His word declares He will never put more on us than we can bear (1 Corinthians 10:13 NIV). Yeah, we know this, but yet it can be so difficult to maintain this perspective when we are in the middle of our trial.

Today, the psalmist brings good news to remind us that even when we encounter many afflictions, God promises to deliver us from each and every one of them! Having "many" afflictions is actually confirmation that you're doing something right and you're on the right path. You see, the enemy only attacks that which intimidates him. If you feel like every time you turn around, there's an arrow coming in your direction, congratulations! You are no longer a baby Christian, and apparently, you are a threat to the kingdom of darkness.

Here is the key though. Do not allow yourself to become distracted or discouraged by the trials. Remember, keep your focus on God! This is done through worship and prayer. When you realize that all of the attacks are really about your kingdom destiny and God fulfilling his purposes through you, you can make it through the middle to the end and finally out of your affliction. Don't let the devil wear you down! In fact, this just might be a great place for you to offer up a praise to God for what he is getting ready to deliver you from!

Scripture Reference: Psalm 34:19 (ESV)

Many are the afflictions of the righteous, but the Lord delivers him out of them all.

Prayer Points: Praise God for His infinite wisdom at work in every circumstance in your life; exalt your God and never your position of frustrations.

In My Own Words: (Construct Your Personalized Prayer):

___

___

___

___

___

___

___

___

___

___

___

___

___

___

___

Faith Declaration: Lord, I praise you today for every affliction I encounter because I know that you are my strong deliverer who rescues me out of them all.

Journal Activity: Have you ever stopped to ask God what lessons He intends for you to learn through your current experience? This is a good place to do so. Now, connect the dots and make the bigger connection. What is it that God has called you to do to impact his kingdom? What is it that you need to be doing even now?

Journaling Notes:

Prayer Confession Day 7: A Prayer for My Pressures

Oh God, I am so grateful that you knew my end at the beginning. Thank you for being in absolute, complete, ultimate control of everything! My times are in your hands. This is a good day to rejoice because I am on your timetable and that deserves my praise.

Father, I can praise you today because I know that I do not have to allow the pressures of life to overtake me. You are my advocate, and I will not give in to the pressures of this world. I will not conform to the systems of men to perform or provide for myself since I am a citizen in your kingdom. It's not up to me to perform perfect works that offer a resolution to all of my problems. It's not up to me to provide my own resources that influence the outcome. No! I will not be tricked by the enemy at attempting to be my own God! I do not have the means in and of myself, but with total abandonment, I look to you.

Instead of leaning on my own understanding, I will yield to the leading and prompting of the precious Holy Spirit to live a life that is in accordance with your will for me. Father, I trust that as I seek you first, you will grant me the desires of my heart. I believe Psalm 62:1-2 that says, "I am at rest in God alone; my salvation comes from Him. He alone is my rock and my salvation, my stronghold; I will never be shaken." Thank you that you alone are the standard by which I live my life, and I will only seek to please you. Thank you for reminding me that you make all things beautiful in your time. I love you, Lord. In Jesus name, I pray, amen.

# ~DAY 8~ God's Got Your Enemies

Scripture Reading: Psalm 3

Humans are one of God's most complex creations. It really is quite fascinating to contemplate how God created us with a free will, giving us the ability to choose. We can choose to submit ourselves to God, or we can choose to submit ourselves to the devil. Just as God uses people to achieve His kingdom purpose, so does the devil work through people to accomplish his for the kingdom of darkness.

This achieving of kingdom purposes can be carried out in different arenas, which we encounter within our everyday lives: our family, our jobs, or even our church. What about our visits to the grocery store, a child's extra-curricular activity, or the mall. Pretty much anywhere you go, you will encounter people. Since everyone has not surrendered their life and will to Christ, this means those individuals are prime candidates to be used by the devil. When this happens, it can become easy to forget that you're really not at war with the person, but rather the spirit at work within the person (Ephesians 6:12).

It is never our job to fight people! It is our place to identify the spirit at work within the person and fight it in the spirit with our spiritual weapons. A true warrior has the ability to identify what's really going on, go into their spiritual arsenal, and utilize the correct weapons to defeat the enemy. You never slay the enemy by resorting to tactics that cause you to "flesh-out."

Oh, you do know what "flesh-out" means, right? It's when you step out of godly character to "go off" on someone instead of maintaining the Fruit of the Spirit. Never allow the tricks of the enemy to cause you to misrepresent who God has called you to be. Keep your witness and your testimony.

I know this can especially be difficult when your character is being assassinated, and the enemy plots lies against you. Just remember that no weapon formed against you shall prosper (Isaiah 54:17). As Christians, we do not empower the devil by relinquishing our self-control. Sometimes you may even have to remind yourself not to take it personally when someone is being used by the devil to oppose you.

Jesus had enemies, and he knew where they were, who they were, and how to handle them. If He was able to overcome, then by His grace, so can we! Whenever you begin to feel overwhelmed and frustrated because of the works of your enemies, just remember, God's got your enemies. So don't you worry; it's not your job to do.

You are an overcomer because the Greater One lives in you (1 John 4:4). You have power over all the works of the devil (Luke 10:19). Pray for those who despitefully misuse you and say all manner of evil against you. Don't worry; great shall be your reward (Matthew 5:11-12). Never hold on to unforgiveness. This way, your heart remains clean and your spirit is free!

<u>Scripture Reference:</u> Psalm 3 (NRSV-in its entirety)

O Lord, how many are my foes! Many are rising against me; many are saying to me, "There is no help for you in God." (Selah) But you, O Lord, are a shield around me, my glory, and the one who lifts up my head. I cry aloud to the Lord, and he answers me from his holy hill. (Selah) I lie down and sleep; I wake again, for the Lord sustains me. I am not afraid of ten thousands of people who have set themselves against me all around. Rise up, O Lord! Deliver me, O my God! For you strike all my enemies on the cheek; you break the teeth of the wicked. Deliverance belongs to the Lord; may your blessing be on your people! (Selah)

Prayer Points: trust God for breakthrough when dealing with the spirit of opposition; believe God for breakthrough and confess it

In My Own Words: (Construct Your Personalized Prayer):

______________________________________________

______________________________________________

______________________________________________

______________________________________________

______________________________________________

______________________________________________

______________________________________________

______________________________________________

______________________________________________

______________________________________________

______________________________________________

______________________________________________

______________________________________________

______________________________________________

______________________________________________

______________________________________________

______________________________________________

______________________________________________

______________________________________________

Faith Declaration: Father, I praise you because you are a shield for me, my glory, and the one who lifts my head above the plans of the enemy. Thank you for breakthrough and for rising up to show yourself strong as my deliverer!

Journal Activity: Pray for every person presenting you with opposition. Call out the spirit you're really dealing with. Take authority over it, and declare breakthrough! After this time of prayer, journal what you sense God saying to you and any instructions he gives.

Journaling Notes:

Prayer Confession Day 8: A Prayer for Breaking the Spirit of Opposition

Lord, thank you for causing me to remember you as Lord of the Breakthrough. I praise you for showing up and showing out on my behalf. What a blessing to know that you are fighting for me! You have gone before me, made crooked places straight, rough places smooth, invaded dark places with your light, and you have brought down every high thing not like you that opposes me!

Thank you for pushing back the kingdom of darkness that the plans and purposes of the enemy will not prevail over yours. Every satanic barrier, assignment, trick, plan, plot, and scheme is destroyed, in the name of Jesus. I decree that the spirit of opposition is broken! It cannot usurp authority over me because your spirit reigns in me. Therefore, I exercise my kingdom dominion and forbid it to operate. The stronghold of opposition will not cause me to act out of character or retaliate. Opposition must bow down to God Almighty!

I declare that the mouth of the enemy is shut! Every lie and negative word spoken against me is null, empty, void, and has no effect on my life. I release to you, Father, every person who has conspired against me and desired my demise. You are so good to me that you even prepare a table for me in their presence. I know that you will deal with them as you see fit. I pray for their hearts to be converted and their spirits to be convicted. I confess that I will walk in love and forgiveness toward them so that I may be free in you. Thank you for being glorified! In Jesus' name, I pray, amen.

# ~DAY 9~
# RELENTLESS FAITH

Scripture Reading: Romans 4:20-22

Repeat these words after me, "I'LL NEVER GIVE UP!" And exactly WHAT are you not giving up on? For starters, God, yourself, and your faith! Abraham is my kind of guy! After all, he does have the distinction of being called "The Father of Many Nations", and the Bible even records that God accounted his faith unto him as righteousness (Genesis 15:6). He must have had some kind of serious faith in God! When warriors are engaged in battle that is NOT the time to lose faith! If you know that God has given you a promise, you must be willing to believe God even when it looks like all is lost.

The word relentless is defined as unyielding; to not soften in feeling, temper, or determination (dictionary.com). Hebrews 11:1 (KJV) tells us, "Now faith is the substance of things hoped for, the evidence of things not seen." Are you fully convinced that God is able to do what he has promised you? What hinders your faith and causes you to waver or doubt if God will come through for you? In order to have relentless faith, you must commit to believing God against all odds. You must have a holy boldness that forces you to remind yourself of who your Daddy is and your relationship with Him. There comes a point that we must resolve within ourselves to believe God. Choosing to believe His promises is the ONLY option for those of us who dare to have faith like a warrior!

In Jeremiah 29:11 (KJV), the prophet proclaims the words of God by saying, "For I know the thoughts that I think toward you, saith the Lord, thoughts of peace, and not of evil, to give you an expected end." God is a good God and a great Father. He is never trying to take something from you, but only trying to get something to you! As your Father, He only has your best interest at heart. We must believe that all things are working together for our good and for His glory because He loves us (Romans 8:28).

God desires to receive maximum glory in our lives, and even our ability to trust and hope in Him brings the Father much glory. We can trust that whatever he has promised us has to come to pass. This is not the time to doubt, waver, or wonder. It is the season to believe God and show forth relentless faith. Does your faith move God? I'm not talking about just believing in faith or believing that God has the power to deliver. But I'm talking about having an abiding assurance within your innermost being that you will receive the promises of God for your life. I declare and join my relentless faith with yours that you shall SEE the victory and behold the promises of God with your own eyes! Hallelujah!!!

Scripture Reference: Romans 4:20-22 (ESV)

No unbelief made him waver concerning the promise of God, but he grew strong in his faith as he gave glory to God, fully convinced that God was able to do what he had promised. That is why his faith was "counted to him as righteousness."

Prayer Points: strength to remain steadfast, hopeful, and stand in faith; faith and trust to be elevated; holy boldness to believe the Word of God and every promise given by God

In My Own Words: (Construct Your Personalized Prayer):

____________________________________________________

____________________________________________________

____________________________________________________

<u>Faith Declaration:</u> Father, today I stand strong in faith, and I will never waver at your promises to me. There is no place for doubt in my heart or mind because I am fully convinced of your faithfulness to me.

<u>Journal Activity:</u> Begin writing a thank you letter to God by faith. Thank him for everything you are believing Him to do in your life as if it is already done. Be specific and name every promise you have relentless faith to believe Him for.

Journaling Notes:

Prayer Confession Day 9: A Prayer for Steadfast Faith

Thank you, Lord, for steadfast faith! I stand unwavering at your promises. I praise you today, in great expectation of receiving radical suddenlies. You have my name assigned to blessings I can't even imagine, and they shall be released to me without delay. It is your good pleasure as a loving Father to provide me with good gifts. I will not be afraid to expect you to come through as you have spoken to me. I will not stagger. I will not doubt. I will not be moved. I am fully persuaded of your faithfulness.

I declare this is my set time of expansion, increase, and blessings. I will live in the overflow of your supernatural provision in every area of my life. The favor of God is ushering me into my wealthy place of tangible manifestations. Nothing is too hard or impossible for you! There is nothing missing, lacking, or fragmented in me. I receive every divine surprise you have purposed especially with me in mind. I will boldly remain steadfast in the confession of my faith to believe you, God!

Thank you for the supernatural harvest of rich rewards released in my life. Thank you for abundant resources for natural and spiritual breakthrough. Thank you for miracles that will bring testimonies of how great you are, and of your exclusive power at work on my behalf. Thank you that my faith is elevated so that I can dream big, ask big, and see the mega poured out upon me. My faith is steadfast and relentless. I have perfect victory. For this, Father, I give you praise. In Jesus' name, amen.

# ~DAY 10~
# MOST POWERFUL LOVE

Scripture Reading: Romans 8:37

The love of God can conquer anything. It's His love that lifts us when we feel we're at our lowest place. It's His love that inspires us to run on and be all He has designed that we should be. It's His love that affirms our identity. It's His love that causes us to believe we will persevere through every obstacle. It's his love that validates our faith in knowing we can safely trust His promises to us.

There is no hardship we could ever encounter that is greater than the love of God. His love is the most powerful love we can ever know. In fact, nothing and no human person could ever love us more completely. His love is empowering, and it causes us to conquer that which seems impossible. When you stop and consider that love compelled God to allow Jesus to die for our reconciliation to Him, how could we not imagine that His love would be enough for us to always conquer every plot of the enemy? It is this empowering, powerful love that assures us victory.

God's love is powerful because it is supernatural. It is literally impossible to comprehend the depth of God's love as it is uniquely expressed to each of His children. His love is covering us like a banner that signifies that we belong to Him. Even when we are drawn to God, it is His love that draws us first. One of the reasons why our personal time of worship should be so intimate is because we are afforded the opportunity to have a personal encounter with God. In His presence, He solidifies his constant, unchanging, never-ending love for us. You have everything you need to make it through your test simply because you are loved by God. To know God and experience His love is the highest, greatest act of living. His love defines who we are; it is our lifeline.

Scripture Reference: Romans 8:37 (NKJV)

Yet in all these things we are more than conquerors through Him who loved us.

Prayer Points: supernatural strength

In My Own Words: (Construct Your Personalized Prayer):

Faith Declaration: Thank you, Lord that because of your powerful love for me, I can conquer anything! I believe you for a supernatural breakthrough!

Journal Activity: In your private time of worship today, bask in the love of God. Let his presence overtake you as you worship Him with abandonment. Now journal about why and all of the ways you love your Father.

Journaling Notes:

Prayer Confession Day 10: A Prayer for Supernatural Strength

Father, I praise you for your supernatural love that gives me supernatural strength. The power of your love strengthens me to conquer anything! Today, I acknowledge my strength as insufficient and lacking. I acknowledge that I need you desperately, and I will not attempt to do anything on my own. May your love guide all I attempt to do as you give me strength.

Thank you that something amazing happens each time I yield to the Holy Spirit. There is tremendous freedom in not having to rely upon myself. I can look to you and lean upon you, Lord. When I feel weak, your strength rises in me. I understand more and more that I am at my best when I am at rest in your love.

I declare your love for me is enough. In fact, it is more than enough of all I need to be assured and confident in who you have called me to be. There is no failure or fear in your love for me. It fills me up and causes me to overflow with your spirit. I praise you because your love secures and steady's my soul. You are my strength, and it is anchored in your love. Thank you, Father. In Jesus' name, I pray, amen.

# ~DAY 11~
# I HAVE A HIDING PLACE

Scripture Reading: Proverbs 18:10

Have you ever noticed the way you feel upon returning home after being gone for several days? No matter how nice the hotel, I always appreciate coming back home to a good night's rest in my own bed. Maybe you get a certain feeling when you're able to return home after a long day of work or just from having dealt with the hustle and bustle of life.

There's just something about turning the key in the door and walking into my house that gives me a sense of safe haven and protection from the cares of this world. Home is the one place you can just be yourself and release your worries. What truly makes a house a home are the people there, the warmth you feel, and the love you encounter in every unique way.

Running into the arms of Jesus is sort of like that feeling of returning home except it's ten times better. Whenever you are engaged in spiritual warfare, it is important to continually look to the hills for your help (Psalm 121:1-2). Even in the midst of the battle, you can take refuge in knowing you have a hiding place in God.

Nothing can overtake you; it doesn't matter how fierce the attack. When God is your strong tower, you will be hidden safely in his arms. Our God is El Elyon, the Most High God. In other words, every spirit is subject to His authority. God is the ultimate defense for the righteous. Since He is our strong tower, we are elevated in His strength, and that makes any enemy a defeated foe.

If the devil has tried to bring intimidation upon you, this is a good time for you to be reminded that you are safe because your strong tower acts as a mighty fortress and will not allow you to be defeated. There is peace in God's presence, so don't be afraid to run to Him. Colossians 3:3 tells us that we are hidden in Christ.

Psalm 91 proclaims that we dwell under the shelter of the Most High God. What wonderful promises to be reminded of and cling to whenever we need extra reassurance from the Word of God. His protection is the greatest buffer you could ask for as you believe God for healing and breakthrough in every area of your life. Go ahead and declare it for yourself, "I am covered because I have a hiding place in Christ!"

Scripture Reference: Proverbs 18:10 (NKJV)

The name of the Lord is a strong tower; the righteous run to it and are safe.

Prayer Points: protection, safety, deliverance, and breakthrough

In My Own Words: (Construct Your Personalized Prayer):

________________________________________

________________________________________

________________________________________

________________________________________

________________________________________

________________________________________

________________________________________

________________________________________

________________________________________

________________________________________

________________________________________

Faith Declaration: Father, I praise you for being my strong tower! No matter what I may encounter, I can run to you, and you keep me safe.

Journal Activity: In what ways have you experienced the protection of God? Consider your answer to expand beyond the physical aspect.

Journaling Notes:

Prayer Confession Day 11: A Prayer for Protection

God, today I confess that you are my hiding place. I praise you because I am fully protected from every arrow and dart sent to me from the kingdom of darkness. Nothing can take me out because you are my fortress! I rejoice because you are my refuge, the one who always keeps me safe from hurt, harm, and danger. Thank you, Lord for the precious blood that never loses its power or ability to keep me covered in your glory.

I declare that I am hidden in my secret place with you. The enemy cannot find me because your hedge of protection encircles me. Under the feathers of your wings, I abide confidently. I cannot be tracked or traced in the spirit realm by any wicked thing because you have preserved me by your grace.

Thank you for deliverance and breakthrough in every battle. Thank you for being my strong tower. I celebrate the greatness of your might and omnipotence. I have peace despite every attack against me. I trust you for it all. In Jesus' name, I pray, amen.

# ~DAY 12~ SPIRITUAL WEAPONS

Scripture Reading: 2 Corinthians 10:2-5

What's worth fighting for? Better yet, who's worth fighting for? At some point, some area of your life is going to be attacked. Tested. Challenged. I hate to be the bearer of bad news, but the reality is, it's inevitable. If it's not your marriage, then maybe it's your parenting, or your health, or your workplace…need I say more? No child of God is exempt from having a target on your back in one season or another. And sometimes, when it rains, it pours, so look out for multiple attacks.

What is the one thing you will not casually stand by and let the enemy invade? Oh, there may be many things we are willing to fight for, but everybody has that one thing that really causes you to go on offense. Something or someone that provokes you to resolve you are going to put the devil on the run before you allow him to bully you with and threaten that which is most important.

For me, it is my daughter. If you are a mother, then I'm sure you can completely relate! I can be the momma bear and the lioness all at the same time if necessary. She is the one person on this earth that I will gladly turn down my plate, fall on my knees, and cry out to God for because I am determined that the enemy will not have her in any way, shape, or form!

As children of God, it is our duty and privilege to pick up our spiritual weapons and fight! Prayer, fasting, praising, worshipping, reading and speaking the Word are just some of the weapons we must keep on hand in our spiritual arsenal. Yes, keep them sharpened and keep them ready.

I have jokingly said on occasion, "I don't look for fights, and I don't start them, but I sure won't back down from one." The truth is, I do start fights. You see, when I finally realized and understood that the devil never fights fair, I figured instead of being in a reactive state, I would be proactive and declare war on him first.

Someone once told me prophetically, "The devil can't stand you, from the moment you wake up and your feet hit the floor." You know why, because praise is how I start my day, and it is one of my greatest weapons. As a matter of fact, before I open my eyes or my mouth, in my mind, I have already started praising God. When I put my feet on the floor, I am giving God glory from within my innermost being. My spirit cries out His praise, and the devil can't stand it because I'm doing what used to be his job.

Since I understand this, I already know, he's going to try and bother me - some way, somehow. But because the Greater One is working on the inside of me and has equipped me with everything I need, I can rejoice that the fight is fixed! He has given me all things pertaining to life and godliness (2 Peter 1:3), and I have power over all the works of the devil (Luke 10:19). God has already gone before us and given us the victory! Today, be confident in your God that He has already won for you the victory, and He will always cause you to triumph ( 2 Corinthians 2:14). Pick up your spiritual weapons and don't be afraid to fight!

<u>Scripture Reference:</u> 2 Corinthians 10:2-5 (NKJV)

For though we walk in the flesh, we do not war according to the flesh. For the weapons of our warfare are not carnal but mighty in God for pulling down strongholds, casting down arguments and every high thing that exalts itself against the knowledge of God, bringing every thought into captivity to the obedience of Christ,

Prayer Points: Pray for wisdom and discernment to utilize spiritual weapons as you engage in warfare for healing and breakthrough.

In My Own Words: (Construct Your Personalized Prayer):

Faith Declaration: Thank you, Father, that I do not wage warfare in my flesh, but I fight in the spirit using my spiritual weapons to pull down strongholds. Everything that would attempt to exalt itself above God is brought down and subject to the authority and power of Christ Jesus.

Journal Activity: First pray about a specific issue you have been battling for a long time. Wait for the Holy Spirit to shed insight to you about the proper strategy to employ. What spiritual weapon (s) do you sense He is telling you to use?

Journaling Notes:

Prayer Confession Day 12: A Prayer for Wisdom and Discernment

Dear Lord, I come before you recognizing that you are the all-wise, omniscient God. Thank you that I can ask you for wisdom and you will liberally give it to me (James 1:5). Thank you that you will not allow me to be ignorant of the devil's devices, but you have empowered me by your spirit to take up my spiritual weapons and fight. I will not shrink back, but I will wage good warfare. You have not given me a spirit of fear, timidity, or weakness. I have the spirit of a warrior!

In the name of Jesus, I declare that my spiritual ears are attuned to your voice, and my spiritual eyes are opened that I may see all you are revealing. I thank you for the spirit of discernment operating in my life through the Holy Spirit. I have the ability to properly discern times and seasons. I decree the wisdom of God is reigning in my mind and over my heart that I will know the strategies God reveals to me with great clarity.

Thank you for teaching me how to be a great warrior and properly utilize every weapon you have given me. I take up my weapon of praise. I take up my weapon of worship. I take up my weapon of prayer and intercession. I take up my weapon of applying the Word of God as I read it and speak it forth. I declare that atmospheres are shifting and environments are changing because the warrior inside of me will always rise to slay! Thank you, Father! In Jesus' name, I pray, amen.

# ~DAY 13~
# GUARANTEED VICTORY

Scripture Reading: 1 Corinthians 15:57

I wish for every person to have one person in this world they can completely depend upon. How wonderful it would be to have that one special person you know will never let you down and always come through just when you need them most. To experience the guarantee of that relationship no matter what, and to know that they will always be there brings a kind of reassurance that you can safely trust and puts your mind at ease.

If you are so blessed, maybe there was someone who immediately came to mind as you just read these words. But for those of you who may have had a difficult time settling within yourself just who that person is, may I offer you the comfort and confidence found in knowing that greater than any guarantee you could ever experience from man, Jesus offers you His personal guarantee to never leave you or forsake you. He also offers you the guarantee of victory through His grace.

The exceptional fact about this spiritual war we are engaged in is how we are guaranteed victory. It's like going to a boxing match that you already know is fixed, and you know from the beginning which contender will ultimately win. So why is it that the devil tries so hard to challenge us over our pre-determined victory? That sneaky, sly enemy understands that the only way we won't experience victory is if we forfeit it ourselves.

Don't relinquish your place of victory in God. Don't release your victory because the devil tries to intimidate and deceive you into believing that he has somehow been exalted above the place of victory God has given you. The enemy specializes in creating distractions and diversions to make us doubt the promises of God for our lives. He may differ in his disguises from one scenario to another, but the reality is they are all smokescreens he uses to lure us into self-doubt that causes us to self-sabotage, which leads to self-defeat.

You might also be wondering, "What about the times I just don't feel victorious?" Thankfully, it is not about how we feel. Remember your feelings can fool you! We walk by faith - not by feelings! Even if in the natural our situation looks bleak and circumstances seem to occur the opposite of the victorious outcome we believe has been promised by God, we must remain steadfast in what we know to be the truth.

The truth of God's word must take preeminence within us. If something takes preeminence, it means it is more important or superior to all others. When the Word of God is preeminent, we will not be fooled by the devil's devices. Our victory has already been bought by the precious blood of Jesus! He now gives us the victory with all rights, privileges, and authority. Stand your ground and maintain your place of victory because it is yours for the taking!

Scripture Reference: 1 Corinthians 15:57 (KJV)

But thanks be to God, which giveth us the victory through our Lord Jesus Christ.

Prayer Points: Declare victory by speaking specifically to every mountain you are facing; speak out what God has promised you concerning your life and call your current situation in alignment with His will.

In My Own Words: (Construct Your Personalized Prayer):

Faith Declaration: Father, I praise you for giving me victory in every situation. Thank you, Jesus, for a supernatural breakthrough!

Journal Activity: What does victory look like for you? Share your faith journey with a godly friend or mentor and don't be afraid to confess to them the victory God has promised you. When you are able to speak it aloud to you are building your faith and aligning your words with what God has already declared. Now, journal about your experience.

Journaling Notes:

Prayer Confession Day 13: A Prayer of Victory

Thank you, Jesus, that your blood gives me authorization to access the victory you have already won for me. I praise you today because I expect the manifestation of what you have declared over my life to evidence with miracles, signs, and wonders. Father, thank you that eyes have not seen, ears have not heard, and neither have minds conceived the great rewards you will bestow upon me, just because you are my loving Father who delights in giving me perfect gifts.

I declare you are the God of supernatural suddenlies. I confess radical suddenlies to be released in every area of my life. I receive by faith sudden healing, sudden blessings, sudden restoration, sudden increase, sudden favor, sudden overflow, sudden deliverance, sudden provision, sudden wealth and riches, sudden divine surprises that are exceedingly, abundantly, and above all I could ever begin to fathom. You are my limitless God with limitless resources to fulfill every promise given to me.

Today is a day of victory! I cannot walk in defeat because your victory resides within me. I decree the devil is under my feet. I am seated in heavenly places with Christ Jesus. The tactics of the enemy are beneath me and aborted by the heavenly hosts of angels God has working on my behalf at his bidding.

Every place I go, I possess territories and take back ground for God's kingdom. I walk in boldness, authority, and victory. I will never succumb to carnal entanglements because I am maintaining my spiritual vision and discernment. I exercise higher-level faith since I live in the glory of God. I know who I am in Christ Jesus. Therefore, I refuse to live beneath my privileges. I triumphantly rise, again and again, as the victor – every time, in every outcome. I win because Jesus has declared my victory, hallelujah! In His precious name, I pray, amen!

# ~DAY 14~
# Do It for Your Glory

Scripture Reading: Isaiah 45:2-3

There are many systems of this world (government, education, business, etc.). All of us at some point or another must engage with the supernatural activity at work within these systems. Each of us is called to infiltrate and impact a particular domain so that the kingdom of God may be revealed. Think about what God has called you to accomplish for His kingdom purposes. Now consider the places you go and the things you do every day. Can you recognize that it is directly connected to your specific kingdom assignment?

When you show up on the scene, you can expect that eventually you will need to deal with the spirit of opposition. The enemy knows how powerful you are and what a threat you possess to his kingdom. He does not want you to effect systemic change for the advancement of the kingdom of God.

Often, God will call us to mountains where his light is needed the most. In the process, we may feel persecution for simply being light in the midst of darkness. The purposes we accomplish and the destiny we fulfill are never about us. Trust and believe, God in His infinite wisdom, definitely has a greater plan. Just as Jesus died to redeem all of mankind back to God, His life mission was so much greater than the pain, suffering, and persecution He experienced in the process. Ultimately, God's plan involves Him getting maximum glory out of us as we are used as His agents of change in every sphere of influence He has established that we should be His ambassadors.

You too will have to overcome much adversity in order to live out your kingdom, daily destiny in God. As his representative in your particular sphere of influence, never forget that you are authorized by God to walk in kingdom authority. Not even the spirit of opposition can overtake you because you are an overcomer. God's grace enables us with the power to walk through any situation we encounter knowing that no matter how trench the warfare, we will emerge victoriously.

Never be moved by people who are used by the enemy to come against you. Remember, our fight is never with flesh, rather it is the spirit at work within people. We must still love them, pray for them, and forgive them so that our spirit remains pure and our conscious free. There may even be instances where it seems really personal, but even then we must be reminded that the war we are waging is supernatural. This is where we rejoice in being confident that God will make crooked places straight, bring down every high thing not like Him, and make what is wrong right because you are the righteousness of God through Christ Jesus.

Always be aware that you wear the name of Christ! He will not allow you to fail because His name is riding on your success. God will never allow you to be overtaken by the enemy. When you pass through the flood, you will not drown, and when you pass through the fire, you shall not even be scorched (Isaiah 43:2). Everything you're contending with is not for your breaking, but really for your making. God knows you can take it because He has gone before you. Since God is fighting for you, do not worry, you have no reason to fear!

In this season, a heavier weight of glory requires that you be tested, even through systemic injustices that you may be confronted with at this time. Nevertheless, God is your advocate. Everything you encounter is necessary because God's glory is being revealed. Since His glory is on the line, you can praise Him for the victory in advance. He will come through for you; He will do it for His glory!

Scripture Reference: Isaiah 45:2-3 (KJV)

I will go before thee, and make the crooked places straight: I will break in pieces the gates of brass, and cut in sunder the bars of iron: And I will give thee the treasures of darkness, and hidden riches of secret places, that thou mayest know that I, the Lord, which call thee by thy name, am the God of Israel.

Prayer Points: Pray that righteousness will be exalted on your behalf and God's sovereign hand at work to deal with the spirit of opposition that would rise against you.

In My Own Words: (Construct Your Personalized Prayer):

Faith Declaration: Thank you, Father, for calling me by name, and thank you for going before me, and bringing down every high thing and crooked place that would try to oppose me.

Journal Activity: Create a prayer list with the names of people you know the enemy is using the spirit of opposition to operate against you. As Christians, we are to sincerely pray for those who spitefully misuse us. Don't allow what you see in the natural to fuel anger or frustration, but use your authority in the spirit to pray on their behalf. Remember to pray scripture and be led by the Holy Spirit in this special time of prayer.

Journaling Notes:

## Prayer Confession Day 14: A Prayer for Righteousness to Be Exalted

Lord, I extol you, exhort you, and exalt your name! Your name is great and greatly to be praised. Your name alone is high and lifted up. Your name alone is worthy, powerful, and honorable. I have the assurance that you will bring me through and lift me above anything that would attempt to keep me in bondage and oppression.

Today, I declare your righteousness to be exalted in every sphere of influence I impact and come into contact with on a daily basis. Where there is wickedness, I pray your light would expel all darkness. May every evil force that would set itself against me be brought to destruction by the authority of your name, your blood, and your Word. I trust you to show up in every situation and move how you see fit. Thank you for dealing with darts meant for my demise. You are the God of justice, and your justice is demonstrated in truth. I can praise you because ultimately, you are in absolute control of everything. I know your justice will reign, hallelujah!

As your blood-bought daughter, I am now your beloved. Since you are my Father and I take on your name, I ask you to exalt your righteousness on my behalf. Where systemic injustices would seek to work against me, I declare that the finished work of Jesus prevails and makes the difference for me. All things are working in my favor. You will not allow any system of this world to trample over me. Instead, I will bring you glory and honor through my godly character as I steadfastly trust you to make all wrongs right.

I choose to rejoice because I believe when it is all said and done, I will come out on top. Not because of my name, but because of yours. Not for my sake, but for the sake of your glory being revealed in me. Lord, do it for your glory! I bless your name and shout the victory now because I believe it is already done! In Jesus' name, I pray, amen.

# ~DAY 15~
# SEND HEAVENLY AID

Scripture Reading: Psalm 108:12-13

There will be times along our Christian journey when we are in the midst of experiences that are too big for us to handle in our own strength, intellect, and knowledge. I like to call these situations "God-size jobs." One of the smartest things we can ever do is realize when we need a miracle and pray for supernatural intervention from God. Sometimes, it's just not expedient to try and logically explain all that is occurring in the spirit realm. You need the wisdom of God to recognize that you need Him to show up and intervene in the matter.

I have been in "tight spots" when the only thing I could utter was, "Jesus Help." I love the scripture reference for today because the psalmist cuts right to the chase. I can almost hear him saying, "God, I can't do this on my own. I need you to send heavenly aid and cause me to enter into victory!" Miracles are not mystical; they are necessary to our faith. I believe there are times when God will allow things to seem as if everything has gone awry so that when he steps in and manifests miracles, we have no choice but to acknowledge that it is the hand of God and God alone. God sets us up, if you will, to experience "God-size jobs" so that there is no way we can take credit for any victory. Instead, we have to testify that "God did it" and point all glory to Him!

As you enter into this week of your journey, I especially want you to be encouraged today. Sometimes, the darkest of night is just before the breaking of day! Even if you cannot see the light at the end of the tunnel right at this moment, rest assured that God is still working on your behalf. Don't be moved by what you do or do not see in the natural. Know that NOTHING is too hard for your God! He is still the God of miracles. He is still the God of breakthrough. He is still the God of victory.

Remember, don't allow worry and wonder to overtake your mind, causing you to doubt if God will show up for you. Your Daddy has already released heavenly aid on your behalf, and the breakthrough of that aid is going to blow your mind! The release of it is just a matter of earth catching up with heaven. As the old song goes, "He may not come when you want Him, but He'll be there right on time." Hold on, do not panic-help is on the way! God's got you covered. You're going through, out and up, in Jesus' name!!!

Scripture Reference: Psalm 108:12-13 (NIV)

Give us aid against the enemy, for human help is worthless. With God, we will gain the victory, and he will trample down our enemies.

Prayer Points: Remain focused and steadfast in God; show forth the fruit of the spirit; pray for others-especially those operating in their flesh or under demonic influences; praise God for broken strongholds.

In My Own Words: (Construct Your Personalized Prayer):

Faith Declaration: I will not rely on human help, but I will depend on the aid of God to trample down my enemies. Today, I have the victory!

Journal Activity: In your journal, make a list of your top seven confessions and make a commitment to intentionally speak them three times a day for the next seven days.

Journaling Notes:

Prayer Confession Day 15: A Prayer of God's Supreme Authority

Father, I praise you with extravagant joy and excitement when I consider your supreme authority. No one is higher or more powerful than you. You have the ability to move heaven and earth, just for me. Mighty are the works of your hand, and none can compare with your exceeding strength as the only true, and living God.

I thank you for assuring me that you have released heavenly aids and interventions on my behalf. You are supernaturally interceding in my life. I believe you have implored a host of angels to intercept every satanic assignment sent to distract, discourage, and destroy me. I thank you for revealing your maximum authority to overrule the plans of hell against my destiny.

Thank you for causing everything to work in my favor by your supernatural power. Every person operating under demonic influence against me is subject to your supreme authority. I will remain fruitful and walk after your spirit so that I do not succumb to my flesh. There is no stronghold that can withstand the supreme authority of God. Thank you, Father, for supernatural, radical, miraculous, divine breakthrough in my life and at work for my advancement. In Jesus' name, I pray, amen.

# ~DAY 16~
# MY GOD IS GREATER

Scripture Reading: Isaiah 54:17

Have you ever stopped to ponder the sheer greatness of God? There is no force bigger, better, stronger, or wiser than Yahweh. He is great, and there is nothing that can be compared to His greatness. No person can surpass His greatness. Yet, His greatness is never diminished because of His love for us. In His decision to share covenant with humanity, it did not impact His ability to simultaneously remain great. The Lord is great above all gods, and the Lord is greatly to be praised (Psalm 96:4).

Weapons come in all types of disguises. Sometimes they are formed in the most unlikely ways, at the most unexpected times, from the most surprising people and circumstances. If we are honest with ourselves, sometimes (maybe not all of the time, but some of the time) we have to admit that we are caught off guard – even if only every once in a while. Whenever we are in a spiritual battle, it is important that we recognize the wiles and weapons of the enemy.

God does not expect us to respond as if the issues we are dealing with are not real. Ignoring the weapon that is formed will not cause you to walk in victory. We should never be ignorantly blissful about our very real situations. Not knowing, understanding, or acknowledging what is occurring in the spirit realm will not make it go away. Make no mistake about it; we are dealing with a real enemy who sends real attacks to disrupt our lives and fellowship with the Father.

The prophet Isaiah records the words of God in our scripture reference today that offers hope. They also serve to warn us that weapons will come. Really, we should not be shaken or out of sorts when we find ourselves under attack. Neither should we be alarmed when false accusations are made against us. This can be especially difficult to accept when we feel as if our character is being assassinated by the lying tongue of others. Nevertheless, we take solace in knowing no matter how fierce the warfare may rage, the promise from God's word is that it will not prosper.

You would think by now the devil would accept defeat. After all this time and after all that has already been said and done by Jesus, he still does not get it. Newsflash: You don't win devil because my God is GREATER!!! And if my God is greater, that means I have the Greater One living down on the inside of me (1 John 4:4). This means I cannot be conquered or defeated because I am destined to win - every time! I don't care how intimidating the weapon, and it doesn't even matter how well devised. The bottom line is, it's already done! I am the victor! I win…because my God is GREATER!!!

Scripture Reference: Isaiah 54:17 (NIV)

"No weapon forged against you will prevail, and you will refute every tongue that accuses you. This is the heritage of the servants of the Lord, and this is their vindication from me," declares the Lord.

Prayer Points: Declare God to be your vindicator; declare breakthrough in every area of your life. Declare victory in every situation you face; believe and stand strong as you boldly voice your faith confessions.

In My Own Words: (Construct Your Personalized Prayer):

Faith Declaration: No matter what weapons may form against me, I have victory in knowing it cannot prosper and prevail over me. Father, thank you for being my vindicator and the one who promises me breakthrough!

Journal Activity: In your prayer time today, target the one weapon the keeps trying to rise up against you. After prayer, record the instructions God gave you about the specific, strategic steps you need to take (spiritually and naturally).

Journaling Notes:

Prayer Confession Day 16: A Prayer of God as Vindicator

All blessing, glory and honor to my great God, who alone is worthy of my praise. Thank you for reminding me that you are my vindicator. I take comfort in the promise of your Word to me that no weapon formed or forged against me can prevail or prosper over me.

Yours exclusively is the greatness, kingdom, and power that rules, reigns, and dominates.

Thank you, Lord, that I operate from a posture of assured victory. I'm not trying to obtain victory because I already have victory! I know my position in relation to you. I live abundantly as a recipient of the privileges you have provided for me. This is my spiritual heritage in you, Father. For this, I give you praise!

I declare that I am spiritually keen and will accurately identify the wiles of the devil so that I may exercise authority over them. Nothing can stop me or block me from excelling in my God-ordained destiny every day of my life. Every hidden attack is exposed; every secret assignment is revealed by the Holy Spirit.

I will not back down, back up, give in, or give up! The enemy will not intimidate me nor make me forfeit my place in God. I rise boldly in the strength of God. My faith is elevated, expanded, and extended to slay the devil with prayers that breakthrough. Thank you, Lord, for fashioning me into your warrior for your glory! In Jesus' name, I pray, amen.

# ~DAY 17~

# ALL MEANS EVERYTHING

Scripture Reading: Romans 8:28

If you love God, and if you are called by God, then that means everything is working together for your good. There is no disclaimer, and there is no contingency clause. So why do we panic and go into "freak out – flip out" mode when bad things happen? It seems so easy to trust God when everything is going well and agreeable to our liking. But when hard, difficult, and ugly things of life confront us, we may tend to wonder, "Where is God in all of this?"

If all means everything, then it is our job to trust God in every situation and season of life. It's kind of what Job meant when he said, "The Lord gives and takes away - blessed be the name of the Lord" (Job1:21). Our trust must be stable, steadfast, constant, and unwavering no matter what challenges we are presented with. Some trials will make you feel as if the wind has just been knocked out of you and there's no way you can be optimistic about any good coming from it. Nevertheless, will you resolve to trust God and believe that He still meant it for your good?

God is not the author of everything that occurs in our lives. However, in His sovereignty and infinite wisdom, He allows everything that happens to serve a purpose of working for our good. When it doesn't look good, sound good, or feel good, it's still for our good.

Remember the three Hebrew boys who were put in a fire roasting furnace? It was for their good. Remember when Daniel was delivered to a lion's den? It was for his good. What about Joseph who was sold into slavery by his own family members? Yep, it was for his good too. Don't forget about David who in different seasons found himself fleeing on the run in attempts to escape his enemy. It was for his good. Or how about Ruth who decided to go to Moab with her mother-in-law Naomi instead of remaining in her native land after the death of her husband? Oh yes, God meant it for her good.

My roll call could go on and on of countless examples of people in the Bible who were tested by what could easily be identified as not so good circumstances on the surface. But when you persevere and get through the shock, heartache, pain, disaster, and trauma, on the other side of it you will be able to look back and realize not only did God bring you through, but it really was for your good all along. In this life, we must learn to accept what God allows. In all that we go through, it is for our good and God's glory!

Scripture Reference: Romans 8:28 (NKJV)

And we know that all things work together for good to those who love God, to those who are the called according to His purpose.

Prayer Points: Praise God for his infinite wisdom at work on your behalf even when you may not understand it; stir your faith to trust and believe God that He is working through everything in this season because it is part of His perfect plan. See the victory and breakthrough first with your spiritual eyes.

In My Own Words: (Construct Your Personalized Prayer):

______________________________________________

______________________________________________

______________________________________________

______________________________________________

______________________________________________

Faith Declaration: Thank you, Lord, that everything that happens in my life is working together for my good and your glory. I can rejoice because you know all things, including my purpose, and you are too wise to make any mistakes. Therefore, I choose to rejoice!

Journal Activity: Recall every terrible event that you have lived through. What were the lessons God meant for you to learn? Can you identify the good that resulted from the events?

Journaling Notes:

Prayer Confession Day 17: A Prayer of Perseverance

Father, when I consider that everything in my life is working together for your greater glory being revealed through me, I can rejoice and give you praise! I have your wisdom, strength, and spiritual perception to know that I am always the victor. My shield of faith covers me and causes me to persevere.

I resolve not to be moved or shaken by what I see going on around me. Thank you for a spirit of endurance. I will not retreat or relinquish. I've come too far not to press forward in you Lord. I refuse to give up, throw in the towel and quit. Nothing gets to dictate my ability to persevere except your Word.

Thank you for reminding me in John 16:33 (NIV), "I have told you these things, so that in me you may have peace. In this world, you will have trouble. But take heart! I have overcome the world." I declare that no matter what, I have your abiding peace through it all because you have already overcome. Since you've overcome, that means so have I! Thank you for this sobering promise.

The joy of the Lord is flooding my soul. It is reminding me that my hope and expectation are in you alone. I will not be disappointed, embarrassed, or humiliated. My God is for me; He is on my side. Thank you, Father! I love you with all of my heart, mind, and will. In Jesus' name, I pray, amen.

# ~DAY 18~
# No Failure In God

Scripture Reading: Psalm 118:13-14

I was pushed back and about to fall…BUT the LORD helped me! What a wonderful testimony on the other side of the test! Yet, how many countless times have I found myself in a predicament where I thought I would fall and consequently, fail? What about you? Do you ever feel as if you are going down for the last count? Do you ever feel like you just can't take one more thing? Do you ever feel as if the wind has been knocked from your sail and you don't have any fight left within you?

Sometimes, our situation can seem so dreary and dismal that it looks like we are going to fail. Despite our best efforts, failure can often seem inevitable. However, it is in these moments we must be reminded that God moves on our behalf DESPITE our best efforts! There is NO failure in God!

In the midst of believing, if we are honest, we can at least admit to ourselves that there are moments we may struggle to stand in faith, consistently confess God's word, and obey God without questioning. Yet, there must be a core conviction that He is worthy of our complete trust because our final resolve is this reassuring truth: God cannot fail.

What does this mean for us? What about the times we absolutely feel like a failure, and there is seemingly tangible evidence to support this claim? Remember what we discussed earlier about feelings? That's right - feelings are fickle, and they will fool you! They also distract you from what's most important, and that is the truth of

God's Word! We do not live nor define our lives by what we feel. Rather, we operate from the position of what we know to be the truth. Truth is only discovered in God's word as you understand your purpose in Him.

If you are really the head and not the tail, if you're really above only and not beneath (Deuteronomy 28:13), then you can't also be a failure. If your identity lies in Christ, then He's in you, and you're in Him.

You are who God says you are, you can do everything God says you can do, and you can have what God says you can. Everything the devil ever told you about your identity is a lie, period! In fact, you are the beautiful opposite of everything the enemy has ever spoken in attempts to label you. You are lovable and loving because God made you worthy. There is no fear of failure that can overtake anything God has already declared about you. Bottom line, If there's no failure in God, then there's no failure in you!

Scripture Reference: Psalm 118:13-14 (NIV)

I was pushed back and about to fall, but the Lord helped me. The Lord is my strength and my defense; he has become my salvation. Shouts of joy and victory resound in the tents of the righteous: "The Lord's right hand has done mighty things! The Lord's right hand is lifted high; the Lord's right hand has done mighty things!" I will not die but live, and will proclaim what the Lord has done.

Prayer Points: Pray for faith to believe confidently that you will SEE and ENTER the victory. Pray to never relent in your trust in our all-powerful God; believe God and expect to SEE and ENTER victory where you are believing God for healing and breakthrough.

In My Own Words: (Construct Your Personalized Prayer):

Faith Declaration: Father, today I praise you and rejoice because you are my help, my strength, and my defense! Thank you for the mighty things you are doing before my eyes. I shall live and NOT die so that I may declare the marvelous works of my God!

Journal Activity: In your journal, write about what it means to persevere and endure when faced with feelings of failure. Think of an instance where you had written yourself off as a failure. How did God reveal to you His perspective and how did it change your perception of yourself?

Journaling Notes:

_______________________________________________

_______________________________________________

_______________________________________________

_______________________________________________

_______________________________________________

_______________________________________________

_______________________________________________

_______________________________________________

_______________________________________________

_______________________________________________

_______________________________________________

_______________________________________________

_______________________________________________

_______________________________________________

_______________________________________________

_______________________________________________

_______________________________________________

_______________________________________________

_______________________________________________

Prayer Confession Day 18: A Prayer of Confidence

Lord, I boldly praise you for the infallible confidence you have given me. You are such a loving Father with great power and great plans for me! Thank you for reminding me nothing is impossible with you; nothing is too difficult for you to handle because there is no failure in you.

I confess you are my help and strength. Thank you for the mighty things you are doing before my eyes. I shall live and NOT die so that I may declare the marvelous works of my God! I confess I will behold and enter into everything you've called me to possess in this life. I have the victory! I believe it's already done, so I can confidently declare that I will demonstrate the tangible evidence of everything you have promised me, even as you are manifesting breakthrough for me!

I choose to reject every lie of the devil. Everything he has ever said to me is a lie. Thank you, Father, I am not a failure! It is impossible for me to fail because Jesus has already assured me victory. I will remain confident in you. Hallelujah! In Jesus' name, I pray, amen.

# ~DAY 19~

## GREATNESS RESIDES ON THE INSIDE

Scripture Reading: Psalm 118:28-35

There is absolutely nothing you can't do that you've been called to accomplish. Do you most assuredly believe that? God has specific kingdom assignments with your name on it and yours alone. He is counting on you to rise up, come forth, and complete the work. Have you considered that His kingdom purposes are bigger than the spiritual warfare that comes along with it?

The only Christians that are not engaging in spiritual warfare are those who are carnal and fruitless. They pose no threat, whatsoever, to the kingdom of darkness. When greatness lives on the inside of you, there are going to be times when you feel as if you must constantly wage "good warfare" as Paul told Timothy (1 Timothy 1:18). In life, we don't get to pick and choose our God-ordained destiny. In God's sovereignty, His purposes for us are according to His will. We cannot pick and choose what we will, or will not say "yes" to through our act of obedience. This is what it means when we surrender and say, "I belong to God."

A wise college mentor once told me, "There is a price we pay for being the person God has called us to be. However, the price we pay for not submitting to being that person is far greater." God gets great glory out of your greatness! Surrendering to His plan and process is not the easiest thing to do. As we are pruned in order that we might bear much fruit, we must remember God allows all of this so that His greatness in us can be revealed.

Daniel 11:32b has become one of my favorite scriptures. It simply states, "…but the people who know their God shall be strong and carry out ***great exploits."*** Isn't it exciting to know that God will allow us to perform great exploits for His honor? In order to do *great* exploits, ***you*** must be pretty *great*!

So often God uses people, places, and things to extract our greatness and let His glory shine through. Never be ashamed of your uniqueness. You are not supposed to flow quite like anyone else, and that's okay! Give yourself permission to be the magnificent, one-of-a-kind, original masterpiece He designed.

If anyone would have told me even three years ago that I would be writing this book, I probably would have laughed aloud, kind of the way Sarah did when God told her she would have a baby at 90 years of age (Genesis 18:12-15). In fact, when the Lord first spoke to my heart about writing this book, my response was the equivalent of what Sarah demonstrated. Although I did not laugh aloud, within myself, I almost immediately dismissed the thought. I responded by going silent…not showing any response or expression…in essence, turning a deaf ear. As if by acting nonresponsive to God, somehow made God mute. Or better yet, now I could feel justified and entitled to pretend as if He had not spoken at all.

Within a matter of days, it was confirmed that this book was indeed on God's radar, even though it was not initially on mine. You see, I've never aspired to be an author. However, sometimes greatness resides so deeply inside of us that we can't recognize it or see it on our own. It takes the love of God to bring forth treasures we have in our earthen vessels (2 Corinthians 4:7). Along our journey, He will also send loving people to help nurture and cultivate that greatness within.

Never allow the uncertainty, unfamiliarity, and uncomfortableness that goes along with birthing greatness allow you to resent or despise whatever your process may look like. Most of all, resist the temptation to compare it to someone else's process. The greater the promise, the greater the struggle. But oh, that I might know Him! Not just in the power of his resurrection, but also in the fellowship of His suffering (Philippians 3:10). Why? Because greatness is within you. Because you are destined for greatness. Because you will do great exploits, all of the glory of God. Remember, not fear, not defeat, but greatness resides inside of you!

Scripture Reference: Psalm 18:28-35 (NIV)

You, Lord, keep my lamp burning; my God turns my darkness into light. With your help I can advance against a troop; with my God, I can scale a wall. As for God, his way is perfect: the Lord's word is flawless; he shields all who take refuge in him. For who is God besides the Lord? And who is the Rock except our God? It is God who arms me with strength and keeps my way secure. He makes my feet like the feet of a deer; he causes me to stand on the heights. He trains my hands for battle; my arms can bend a bow of bronze. You make your saving help my shield, and your right hand sustains me; your help has made me great.

Prayer Points: Make my feet like the feet of deer that I might ascend into the high places of God.

In My Own Words: (Construct Your Personalized Prayer):

Faith Declaration: It is you oh God, who keeps my lamp burning, who arms me with strength, and sustains me by your right hand. I praise you for victory and breakthrough!

Journal Activity: What is it that God has told you to do that you haven't done yet? Why? How will this change? When? Give God another opportunity by confessing your desire to say "yes" to the greatness he has placed inside of you being uncovered for His greater glory.

Journaling Notes:

Prayer Confession Day 19: A Prayer to Activate and Release Greatness

Lord, thank you for reminding me today just how much greatness resides in me. I am your daughter. Since you are a great God, that means I have your DNA in me. Help me to recognize what is sometimes difficult to identify in myself although it is often easy to identify in others. Give me a greater resolve to fully embrace the greatness you've called me to live out.

Today, I acknowledge and accept every seed of greatness you have already deposited within me. I am a great person, just like my heavenly Father. I can do great exploits for your kingdom. I will not be intimidated by the magnitude of greatness you have called me to, but I will endeavor to approach it in humility and your grace.

I declare I can do all things through your strength and power. I declare that you make my feet like that of deer and have given me hinds feet for high places (Psalm 18:33). I declare I shall accomplish great exploits for you. I know you, I praise you, and I love you. In Jesus' name, I pray, amen.

# ~DAY 20~
# GRACED TO WAIT

Scripture Reading: Psalm 27:13-14

As you continue to trust God for healing and breakthrough in every area of your life, I want you to be reminded that you have been given a special grace to believe by faith and wait upon God for his perfect timing of manifestation. Because of this grace, it allows you to rest in God instead of being anxious over the delivery of His promises. We only begin to faint when we cease to believe that we are already victorious.

As you begin to approach the end of your devotional journey, you may be thinking, "I do not have the healing and breakthrough in those areas I have petitioned God about." Maybe you don't. You see, there's nothing magical about the numbers 21 or 31, even in the context of a special fast, time of prayer, or a devotional journey such as this one. Let me explain.

We are often product-outcome oriented, and God is often process-outcome oriented. In other words, the journey was not so much about the changes you've asked God for through your healing and breakthrough. The journey was most importantly about "the you on the inside" that needed to change and make adjustments in order to see Jesus revealed in your life in this present season - yes, through every situation and circumstance so that you can receive all the Father has for you. This book was just the vehicle to moving you closer to that posture so that you're able to receive the healing and breakthrough God has for you in various aspects of your life.

The beautiful thing about grace is that we are empowered by the Holy Spirit to wait with great expectancy and not lose heart. We can abide in the Fruit of the Spirit (Galatians 5:22-23) because we have God's grace to wait upon Him. Our hope and expectation is from God and God alone - not people or things. Our hope will not be disappointed or put to shame or confusion if we can just wait in grace upon our Father (Romans 5:5, Psalm 31:1).

So, be encouraged and do not be weary in well doing, for in due season you will reap if you faint not (Galatians 6:9). Don't faint! Don't worry and don't wonder about the who, what, when, where, why, and how so much that it becomes your focus instead of your faith. Do not let your thoughts drift away from the presence of God. God has a good plan for your life filled with good things because of His goodness. You have an expected end! (Jeremiah 29:11).

All of your hurt, pain, and disappointment has a divine purpose. It's not all been for nothing! God wastes nothing, and He uses everything! Step by step, it has brought you closer to the fulfillment of your destiny. Your life has significant value to God. This is why He wants us to experience abundant life in Him. Every day we choose to live on purpose in obedience to His will for us.

Even when things don't look the way we think they should or seem right to us, be confident that God is right on schedule. His timing really is perfect. May He give you more grace to believe, trust and hope in Him without fail. And when you think you can't take one more thing a minute longer, just remind yourself, "I've been graced to wait."

<u>Scripture Reference:</u> Psalm 27:13-14 (KJV)

I had fainted, unless I had believed to see the goodness of the Lord in the land of the living. Wait on the Lord: be of good courage, and he shall strengthen thine heart: wait, I say, on the Lord.

Prayer Points: Praise God for the ability to trust His faithfulness; praise God for increased faith. Praise God for every word he has spoken, and put Him in remembrance of His promises to you.

In My Own Words: (Construct Your Personalized Prayer):

Faith Declaration: I will not faint, but I will take courage as I wait upon the Lord in faith. My heart is strengthened because I believe that I shall see his promises to me revealed!

Journal Activity: What does being "graced to wait" mean to you in this season of your life? Is there any anxiety you have over fully trusting God? Do you completely have peace as you hope in God? If you are not fully trusting and resting in God's peace, what is it you sense God prodding you to do so that your hope in Him is not shaken?

Journaling Notes:

## Prayer Confession Day 20: A Prayer of Courage

Dear Lord, thank you for giving me courage to wait in grace as I yet believe you to manifest every promise for healing and breakthrough in my life. I confess your courage to wait in peace and patience with great joy. I can confidently display courage to trust you as I wait because I know that everything has already been done!

I declare I have the courage to keep speaking life to my situation. I declare I have the courage to keep believing you for the fulfillment of every promise you've given me. I declare I have the courage to keep expecting the glory of God to be revealed on my behalf despite my present circumstances. I declare I have the courage to obey you even when it doesn't make sense to me or others. I declare I have the courage to stand strong in my relentless faith, anchored in your Word.

Just as you told Joshua multiple times to only be strong and very courageous, I too understand this is what I must do in order to access what you have already reserved for me. I boldly confess that I am possessing everything you've designated for me. There is no place for, and I refuse to give in to doubt, depression, disgust, discouragement, and disappointment. The warrior in me will stand up, every single time! Thank you, Lord, for how you have changed me through this process. I am graced to wait with great courage. In Jesus' name, I pray, amen.

# ~DAY 21~
# REJOICE IN PRAISE

Scripture Reading: Psalm 119:165

Well. Guess what? You did it! You made it to Day twenty-one, and now it's time to celebrate! Celebrate the fact that God is faithful; celebrate the fact that God rewards those who diligently seek Him. Celebrate the fact that every point along this journey has made you stronger, wiser, and closer in your relationship with God. Your praise is symbolic of your victories - past, present, and future.

As we recount all the past moments when God has already blessed us, it provokes us to praise Him even more. Sometimes we are overwhelmingly aware of the blessings He is bestowing upon us even now, and we can't help but to praise Him. Other times, we praise God in advance for all that we are believing for and have not yet received, but still remain convinced that He will come through (remember…it's already done!). We are always cycling through these phases, but nevertheless, we abound in our conviction to rejoice in the Lord - always (Philippians 4:4).

Praising God is one sure way to enter into His presence. God's presence brings stability, clarity, and peace. When you are anchored in God, nothing can unravel your confidence or disturb your composure. Your praise is a witness of your total assurance that God is your healer and the source of your breakthrough. Praising God touches the heart of the Father because He is moved by our faith.

Our praise gets His attention unlike any other way we commune with Him. It brings Him great joy that we make the choice to praise Him and are not dictated and controlled by our feelings (which are always subject to change). This consistent choice and attitude of praise becomes who we are at our core, not just an outward action or response.

God is worthy of our praise and adoration not just because of what He does but simply because of who He is. We must always appreciate and value His presence in our lives above any tangible thing, or even the manifestation of everything we desire. While seasons will always change, our praise must remain a permanent fixture in the fabric of our lives. Praise helps us to keep our priority on being with God, no matter what we are going through or dealing with.

My prayer for you is that every day of your life will be like day twenty-one…days of rejoicing in praise! Let praise always be your first action and reaction of the day. May it arise within you so greatly that it becomes bigger than anything else. The Bible says, "Praise is comely to the upright" (Psalm 33:1). In other words, let this be your automatic, natural response to God.

It is hard to complain about anything when your mouth is filled with praise. Allow your praise to reinforce your faith. Lose yourself in God's presence. Forsake all inhibitions, schisms, skeptics, and (dare I say) critics that would try to minimize your praise. Never allow anyone to put the "praiser" within you inside a little box, neatly compartmentalized into the back corner of their mind's perception of how you should praise your God.

I challenge you to abandon and break out of the norm, and even your own comfort zone, because there is something so powerful about praising God that it can't be explained. Instead, it has to be experienced. Today, seal everything you've been believing for with a praise! Watch and wait, believe and receive - He's done what you thought was difficult, hard, and impossible. Your healing is here! Your breakthrough is here! Don't stop rejoicing, and don't stop giving your God all of your praise!

Scripture Reference: Psalm 119:165 (ESV)

Great peace have those who love your law; nothing can make them stumble.

Prayer Points: Praise God for his complete healing and victory in every area of your life.

In My Own Words: (Construct Your Personalized Prayer):

Faith Declaration: Thank you, Father, for your peace that comes from your Word. Nothing will cause me to fall because I am rooted and grounded in you, and because you have lifted me up through your powerful love.

Journal Activity: Take time out to be with God today in particular and offer up a special praise. Journal about your praise experience during your devotional time today.

Journaling Notes:

Prayer Confession Day 21: A Prayer of Praise

Father, I praise you! You alone are worthy of my highest and best praise. When I consider who you are, and how you love me, I am completely overwhelmed! Your presence fills me completely. For this, I give you praise.

I know that everything that has been spoken from me to you, and you to me over the past twenty-one days has changed me for your glory. I am now in a place to receive what you have for me in a way I could not have fully embraced before. The journey has been for my good, and I am so grateful. I praise you for healing and breakthrough in every area of my life!

I am rooted in your Word, and I will never stop praising you for being my God, my Father, my Friend, and my Deliverer! You are always faithful to me! I am a warrior! Your daughter, but a warrior none the less. I win every time I worship! I slay every opposition every time I pray!

As I take the next ten days to deeply reflect upon and process all that has occurred over the past twenty-one days, I know you are going to continue to meet me at every turn and point. Thank you that I abide in you and you abide in me. I will never cease to rejoice in you and give you praise. In Jesus' name, I pray, amen.

The second half of this devotional book is designed to help you solidify everything you have encountered in the first half. Please follow the outline below to complete this devotional journey for days 22-31.

> Days 22: Today is your make up day! If there are any days you need to go back to and finish reading or re-read, this is your opportunity to catch up.
>
> Day 23: Today is your day to finish and review all of your journal entries. Meditate on the revelations that come from the Holy Spirit.

Day 24: Today is your day to finish constructing your own personal prayers. Take this time to reflect upon what God pours into your heart as you write them out.

Day 25: Today is your day to read aloud your personal constructed prayers from days 1-7.

Day 26: Today is your day to read aloud your personal constructed prayers from days 8-14.

Day 27: Today is your day to read aloud your personal constructed prayers from days 15-21.

Day 28: Today is your day to review all of the faith declaration statements and speak them over yourself.

Day 29: Today is the day to read aloud the prayer confessions from the book for days 1-7.

Day 30: Today is the day to read aloud the prayer confessions from the book for days 8-14.

Day 31: Today is the day to read aloud the prayer confessions from the book for days 15-21.

Now be reminded once more, you are the warrior who will always win in worship and slay every time you pray. Warrior SLAY!

# Appendix of Daily Prayers

**Prayer Confession Day 1: A Prayer for Restoration**

Heavenly Father, I begin this devotional journey today by giving you praise. I confess that you are good, gracious, worthy, and wise. Thank You for this opportunity to come into your presence with a heart, mind, and mouth filled with your praise.

I come to you transparent, withholding nothing, spiritually naked and vulnerable. I recognize that you are the one and only person I can be completely broken before. Yet, you will not reject me. As your daughter, I acknowledge that I need you desperately. The thought of doing life without you or even on my own terms is completely meaningless. I am eternally grateful that you made a way for me to experience your love through Jesus. I am so glad I can have my own relationship with you.

Today, I ask you to restore me. Every place within me that needs your touch, I pray that you would breathe on me. Even right now, I repent of my sin, and I ask you to cleanse me. Give me a heart and mind that wants to obey your Word and surrender to your plan for my life. Help me to submit even in the areas I have struggled to relinquish control. I realize this is necessary so that I can be made whole in you.

Holy Spirit, restore my joy, my strength, and my will to be the woman you have called me to be. Restore my spirit that has been worn and weary from the cares of this world. Where I have been crushed by frustration, distracted by disappointments, and overwhelmed by my own inadequacies – where I have believed lies from the enemy and proven negligent in my ability to recover on my own - today I cry out to you, Lord! Help me! Father, restore my soul. Lead me in paths of righteousness for your name's sake. Guide me into refreshing green pastures. Instead of being overtaken by rushing waters that would overwhelm my soul, allow me to drink from them calmly. Help me to remember that you are my living well and the only source that will never run dry. In Jesus' name, I pray, amen.

### Prayer Confession Day 2: A Prayer for Focus

Father, today I choose to praise you on purpose! I will not be moved by people around me, my circumstances, or even my own feelings. Despite the challenges I face in my body, in my relationships, in my finances, in my emotions, and in my mind, I still choose to submit myself completely to you. I decree by my own words my commitment, nevertheless, to remain focused on you! I know that you hear me and save me every time I cry out to you. Rescue me from any sickness in my body, illness in my thoughts, and ailments in my emotions. I confess that you are my God and my healer.

I believe your word in 2 Thessalonians 3:3 (NIV) that says, "The Lord is faithful, and he will strengthen and protect you from the evil one." Lord, no matter what the enemy may attempt to do to break my focus, I trust you to protect and guard me from every attack. I declare that my eyes are fixed upon you. I will not be moved by distractions. I declare that I stand strong in faith because I stand strong in you, holding fast to your Word that cannot return unto you void.

I can praise you for unshakable, unstoppable, and unsinkable, faith despite tests and trials that confront me. I will not be afraid! When the storm blows over, I will still be standing in you. I choose to rest in you as an act of my faith and obedience to your Word. Yes, I believe that I will live to see the goodness of the Lord in the land of the living as I daily live in your presence. In Jesus 'name, I pray, amen.

### Prayer Confession Day 3: A Prayer for Healing

Lord, thank you for being my healer. I refuse to believe, accept, or confess anything else over my life. I believe in the power of speaking your Word over myself. I know you have given me this power to exercise great faith! Thank you that no situation is too difficult for you, and despite what I may feel, even in my body, I know that you are working in my circumstances. Manifestation of breakthrough and healing is mine!

I am grateful for medical expertise that you have provided to me. I am also grateful that you have educated me to understand the difference between facts and truth. Regardless of what the facts may be, the truth of the matter is by the stripes of Jesus, I am already healed! According to Isaiah 53:5 (NKJV): "Jesus was wounded for our transgressions, He was bruised for our iniquities; the chastisement for our peace was upon Him, and by His stripes we are healed." Jesus is my great physician, hallelujah!

I confess that I am healed from all minor sickness and life-threatening disease that would attempt to afflict my body. Every physical ailment, terminal illness, chronic symptom, and occasional sickness is subject to the authority of the blood of Jesus. Pain is not my portion! I receive the relief of God that comes from your healing virtue to permeate and penetrate every place where I hurt.

My body is healed and whole. It shall function as it has been designed to function. There is nothing missing or lacking in my health. My body is the temple of the Holy Spirit, and it will be in perfect alignment that God may be glorified in me. I declare my healing, and it's in Jesus' name, I pray, amen.

## Prayer Confession Day 4: A Prayer of Reassurance

Father, as I reflect and remember, I can praise you for your faithfulness to me. There has never been a time in my life you were not with me. Thank you for reminding me of your steadfast love for me. I have no doubt that you are moving in my midst today and working through my situation for my good. You are a good Father with good gifts and plans for me. I won't be moved by what I encounter in the natural because it is temporary and subject to change at any moment.

Today, I confess that your track record and credit are perfect. I am securely reassured that as I continue to worship and pray; I am that much closer to receiving the healing and breakthrough you have already freely given me. I declare manifestation is on the way! Just because I may not have it at this moment does not mean it will not suddenly show up. I expect to see your glory on display on my behalf. As I wait in you, I access memories of what you've already done for me, and how time after time, you've proven yourself to me. This is why I can rejoice! This is why I can remain hopeful and full of faith! This is why I choose to praise you. I command the warrior on the inside of me to arise! In Jesus' name, I pray, amen.

## Prayer Confession Day 5: A Prayer for Renewed Strength

Father, thank you for reminding me today that I am stronger than I have realized. I am still here in the land of the living to call out to you. That means you are sustaining and maintaining me, despite what I may see in the natural or how I may even feel or think. I confess today that your strength is lifting me above anything that would seek to hold me down. For this, Father, I can offer you praise!

I declare out of my own mouth that I will persevere in faith by your grace. I refuse to give up, and I will not quit. I am anointed to finish strong and stand fast in the confession of my faith. Everything you have promised me shall come to pass. When I feel like I am about to faint, fall, or falter, your strength will refresh me. I will wait patiently for your perfect timing to manifest the deliverance, healing, and breakthrough you've already given me. It must materialize because you have declared it to be so according to your Word.

Thank you for your power that causes me to trust you and rest in you today. Thank you for your power that causes me to keep going. Thank you for your power to speak the right words in my circumstance or even a negative situation. Thank you for your mighty power that reminds me you are a mighty God. I am strong in you, and I receive renewed strength this day. In Jesus' mighty name I pray, amen.

## Prayer Confession Day 6: A Prayer for Living in the Word

Lord, I praise you for your Word! I renew my commitment to live in your Word consistently. I ask that you would help me to cherish being with you above all else. Whatever stops me from fully receiving your Word, please remove it from me. Do not allow anything to distract me from spending time each day reading, meditating, or studying your Word. Help me to value it in such a way that reading the Bible is a high priority in my lifestyle. I resolve to make time to be in the Word because the Word of God is foundational to my spiritual growth.

I confess that I am deeply anchored in your Word. In the face of difficulty, I cannot be moved because your Word is hidden in my heart. I am destined to emerge victorious and triumphant because of the authority of your Word. Psalm 119:130 (NLT) declares, "The teaching of your Word gives light, so even the simple can understand." There is no issue in my life that your Word cannot handle. I thank you for the power, direction, and clarity that comes with your Word. I boldly proclaim your Word over my life this day. It will have the final authority over all that governs my actions and reactions. I will not be moved or shaken because your Word makes me secure.

Thank you, Father, for sending your Word to heal me and make me whole in every aspect of my life. Thank you that your Word ministers deliverance to my soul. There is no destruction that can befall me that is greater than your Word! Your Word is true because you are true. I firmly stand with assurance upon your Word, active and alive in me! In Jesus's name I pray, amen.

## Prayer Confession Day 7: A Prayer for My Pressures

Oh God, I am so grateful that you knew my end at the beginning. Thank you for being in absolute, complete, ultimate control of everything! My times are in your hands. This is a good day to rejoice because I am on your timetable and that deserves my praise.

Father, I can praise you today because I know that I do not have to allow the pressures of life to overtake me. You are my advocate, and I will not give in to the pressures of this world. I will not conform to the systems of men to perform or provide for myself since I am a citizen in your kingdom. It's not up to me to perform perfect works that offer a resolution to all of my problems. It's not up to me to provide my own resources that influence the outcome. No! I will not be tricked by the enemy at attempting to be my own God! I do not have the means in and of myself, but with total abandonment, I look to you.

Instead of leaning on my own understanding, I will yield to the leading and prompting of the precious Holy Spirit to live a life that is in accordance with your will for me. Father, I trust that as I seek you first, you will grant me the desires of my heart. I believe Psalm 62:1-2 that says, "I am at rest in God alone; my salvation comes from Him. He alone is my rock and my salvation, my stronghold; I will never be shaken." Thank you that you alone are the standard by which I live my life, and I will only seek to please you. Thank you for reminding me that you make all things beautiful in your time. I love you, Lord. In Jesus name, I pray, amen.

**Prayer Confession Day 8: A Prayer for Breaking the Spirit of Opposition**

Lord, thank you for causing me to remember you as Lord of the Breakthrough. I praise you for showing up and showing out on my behalf. What a blessing to know that you are fighting for me! You have gone before me, made crooked places straight, rough places smooth, invaded dark places with your light, and you have brought down every high thing not like you that opposes me!

Thank you for pushing back the kingdom of darkness that the plans and purposes of the enemy will not prevail over yours. Every satanic barrier, assignment, trick, plan, plot, and scheme is destroyed, in the name of Jesus. I decree that the spirit of opposition is broken! It cannot usurp authority over me because your spirit reigns in me. Therefore, I exercise my kingdom dominion and forbid it to operate.

The stronghold of opposition will not cause me to act out of character or retaliate. Opposition must bow down to God Almighty!

I declare that the mouth of the enemy is shut! Every lie and negative word spoken against me is null, empty, void, and has no effect on my life. I release to you, Father, every person who has conspired against me and desired my demise. You are so good to me that you even prepare a table for me in their presence. I know that you will deal with them as you see fit. I pray for their hearts to be converted and their spirits to be convicted. I confess that I will walk in love and forgiveness toward them so that I may be free in you. Thank you for being glorified! In Jesus' name, I pray, amen.

## Prayer Confession Day 9: A Prayer for Steadfast Faith

Thank you, Lord, for steadfast faith! I stand unwavering at your promises. I praise you today, in great expectation of receiving radical suddenlies. You have my name assigned to blessings I can't even imagine, and they shall be released to me without delay. It is your good pleasure as a loving Father to provide me with good gifts. I will not be afraid to expect you to come through as you have spoken to me. I will not stagger. I will not doubt. I will not be moved. I am fully persuaded of your faithfulness.

I declare this is my set time of expansion, increase, and blessings. I will live in the overflow of your supernatural provision in every area of my life. The favor of God is ushering me into my wealthy place of tangible manifestations. Nothing is too hard or impossible for you! There is nothing missing, lacking, or fragmented in me. I receive every divine surprise you have purposed especially with me in mind. I will boldly remain steadfast in the confession of my faith to believe you, God!

Thank you for the supernatural harvest of rich rewards released in my life. Thank you for abundant resources for natural and spiritual breakthrough. Thank you for miracles that will bring testimonies of how great you are, and of your exclusive power at work on my behalf. Thank you that my faith is elevated so that I can dream big, ask big, and see the mega poured out upon me. My faith is steadfast and relentless. I have perfect victory. For this, Father, I give you praise. In Jesus' name, amen.

**Prayer Confession Day 10: A Prayer for Supernatural Strength**

Father, I praise you for your supernatural love that gives me supernatural strength. The power of your love strengthens me to conquer anything! Today, I acknowledge my strength as insufficient and lacking. I acknowledge that I need you desperately, and I will not attempt to do anything on my own. May your love guide all I attempt to do as you give me strength.

Thank you that something amazing happens each time I yield to the Holy Spirit. There is tremendous freedom in not having to rely upon myself. I can look to you and lean upon you, Lord. When I feel weak, your strength rises in me. I understand more and more that I am at my best when I am at rest in your love.

I declare your love for me is enough. In fact, it is more than enough of all I need to be assured and confident in who you have called me to be. There is no failure or fear in your love for me. It fills me up and causes me to overflow with your spirit. I praise you because your love secures and steady's my soul. You are my strength, and it is anchored in your love. Thank you, Father. In Jesus' name, I pray, amen.

**Prayer Confession Day 11: A Prayer for Protection**

God, today I confess that you are my hiding place. I praise you because I am fully protected from every arrow and dart sent to me from the kingdom of darkness. Nothing can take me out because you are my fortress! I rejoice because you are my refuge, the one who always keeps me safe from hurt, harm, and danger. Thank you, Lord for the precious blood that never loses its power or ability to keep me covered in your glory.

I declare that I am hidden in my secret place with you. The enemy cannot find me because your hedge of protection encircles me. Under the feathers of your wings, I abide confidently. I cannot be tracked or traced in the spirit realm by any wicked thing because you have preserved me by your grace.

Thank you for deliverance and breakthrough in every battle. Thank you for being my strong tower. I celebrate the greatness of your might and omnipotence. I have peace despite every attack against me. I trust you for it all. In Jesus' name, I pray, amen.

## Prayer Confession Day 12: A Prayer for Wisdom and Discernment

Dear Lord, I come before you recognizing that you are the all-wise, omniscient God. Thank you that I can ask you for wisdom and you will liberally give it to me (James 1:5). Thank you that you will not allow me to be ignorant of the devil's devices, but you have empowered me by your spirit to take up my spiritual weapons and fight. I will not shrink back, but I will wage good warfare. You have not given me a spirit of fear, timidity, or weakness. I have the spirit of a warrior!

In the name of Jesus, I declare that my spiritual ears are attuned to your voice, and my spiritual eyes are opened that I may see all you are revealing. I thank you for the spirit of discernment operating in my life through the Holy Spirit. I have the ability to properly discern times and seasons. I decree the wisdom of God is reigning in my mind and over my heart that I will know the strategies God reveals to me with great clarity.

Thank you for teaching me how to be a great warrior and properly utilize every weapon you have given me. I take up my weapon of praise. I take up my weapon of worship. I take up my weapon of prayer and intercession. I take up my weapon of applying the Word of God as I read it and speak it forth. I declare that atmospheres are shifting and environments are changing because the warrior inside of me will always rise to slay! Thank you, Father! In Jesus' name, I pray, amen.

**Prayer Confession Day 13: A Prayer of Victory**

Thank you, Jesus, that your blood gives me authorization to access the victory you have already won for me. I praise you today because I expect the manifestation of what you have declared over my life to evidence with miracles, signs, and wonders. Father, thank you that eyes have not seen, ears have not heard, and neither have minds conceived the great rewards you will bestow upon me, just because you are my loving Father who delights in giving me perfect gifts.

I declare you are the God of supernatural suddenlies. I confess radical suddenlies to be released in every area of my life. I receive by faith sudden healing, sudden blessings, sudden restoration, sudden increase, sudden favor, sudden overflow, sudden deliverance, sudden provision, sudden wealth and riches, sudden divine surprises that are exceedingly, abundantly, and above all I could ever begin to fathom. You are my limitless God with limitless resources to fulfill every promise given to me.

Today is a day of victory! I cannot walk in defeat because your victory resides within me. I decree the devil is under my feet. I am seated in heavenly places with Christ Jesus. The tactics of the enemy are beneath me and aborted by the heavenly hosts of angels God has working on my behalf at his bidding.

Every place I go, I possess territories and take background for God's kingdom. I walk in boldness, authority, and victory. I will never succumb to carnal entanglements because I am maintaining my spiritual vision and discernment. I exercise higher-level faith since I live in the glory of God. I know who I am in Christ Jesus. Therefore, I refuse to live beneath my privileges. I triumphantly rise, again and again, as the victor – every time, in every outcome. I win because Jesus has declared my victory, hallelujah! In His precious name, I pray, amen!

**Prayer Confession Day 14: A Prayer for Righteousness to Be Exalted**

Lord, I extol you, exhort you, and exalt your name! Your name is great and greatly to be praised. Your name alone is high and lifted up. Your name alone is worthy, powerful, and honorable. I have the assurance that you will bring me through and lift me above anything that would attempt to keep me in bondage and oppression.

Today, I declare your righteousness to be exalted in every sphere of influence I impact and come into contact with on a daily basis. Where there is wickedness, I pray your light would expel all darkness. May every evil force that would set itself against me be brought to destruction by the authority of your name, your blood, and your Word. I trust you to show up in every situation and move how you see fit. Thank you for dealing with darts meant for my demise. You are the God of justice, and your justice is demonstrated in truth. I can praise you because ultimately, you are in absolute control of everything. I know your justice will reign, hallelujah!

As your blood-bought daughter, I am now your beloved. Since you are my Father and I take on your name, I ask you to exalt your righteousness on my behalf. Where systemic injustices would seek to work against me, I declare that the finished work of Jesus prevails and makes the difference for me. All things are working in my favor. You will not allow any system of this world to trample over me. Instead, I will bring you glory and honor through my godly character as I steadfastly trust you to make all wrongs right.

I choose to rejoice because I believe when it is all said and done, I will come out on top. Not because of my name, but because of yours. Not for my sake, but for the sake of your glory being revealed in me. Lord, do it for your glory! I bless your name and shout the victory now because I believe it is already done! In Jesus' name, I pray, amen.

**Prayer Confession Day 15: A Prayer of God's Supreme Authority**

Father, I praise you with extravagant joy and excitement when I consider your supreme authority. No one is higher or more powerful than you. You have the ability to move heaven and earth, just for me. Mighty are the works of your hand, and none can compare with your exceeding strength as the only true, and living God.

I thank you for assuring me that you have released heavenly aids and interventions on my behalf. You are supernaturally interceding in my life. I believe you have implored a host of angels to intercept every satanic assignment sent to distract, discourage, and destroy me. I thank you for revealing your maximum authority to overrule the plans of hell against my destiny.

Thank you for causing everything to work in my favor by your supernatural power. Every person operating under demonic influence against me is subject to your supreme authority. I will remain fruitful and walk after your spirit so that I do not succumb to my flesh. There is no stronghold that can withstand the supreme authority of God. Thank you, Father, for supernatural, radical, miraculous, divine breakthrough in my life and at work for my advancement. In Jesus' name, I pray, amen.

**Prayer Confession Day 16: A Prayer of God as Vindicator**

All blessing, glory and honor to my great God, who alone is worthy of my praise. Thank you for reminding me that you are my vindicator. I take comfort in the promise of your Word to me that no weapon formed or forged against me can prevail or prosper over me. Yours exclusively is the greatness, kingdom, and power that rules, reigns, and dominates.

Thank you, Lord, that I operate from a posture of assured victory. I'm not trying to obtain victory because I already have victory! I know my position in relation to you. I live abundantly as a recipient of the privileges you have provided for me. This is my spiritual heritage in you, Father. For this, I give you praise!

I declare that I am spiritually keen and will accurately identify the wiles of the devil so that I may exercise authority over them. Nothing can stop me or block me from excelling in my God-ordained destiny every day of my life. Every hidden attack is exposed; every secret assignment is revealed by the Holy Spirit.

I will not back down, back up, give in, or give up! The enemy will not intimidate me nor make me forfeit my place in God. I rise boldly in the strength of God. My faith is elevated, expanded, and extended to slay the devil with prayers that breakthrough. Thank you, Lord, for fashioning me into your warrior for your glory! In Jesus' name, I pray, amen.

## Prayer Confession Day 17: A Prayer of Perseverance

Father, when I consider that everything in my life is working together for your greater glory being revealed through me, I can rejoice and give you praise! I have your wisdom, strength, and spiritual perception to know that I am always the victor. My shield of faith covers me and causes me to persevere.

I resolve not to be moved or shaken by what I see going on around me. Thank you for a spirit of endurance. I will not retreat or relinquish. I've come too far not to press forward in you Lord. I refuse to give up, throw in the towel and quit. Nothing gets to dictate my ability to persevere except your Word.

Thank you for reminding me in John 16:33 (NIV), "I have told you these things, so that in me you may have peace. In this world, you will have trouble. But take heart! I have overcome the world." I declare that no matter what, I have your abiding peace through it all because you have already overcome. Since you've overcome, that means so have I! Thank you for this sobering promise.

The joy of the Lord is flooding my soul. It is reminding me that my hope and expectation are in you alone. I will not be disappointed, embarrassed, or humiliated. My God is for me; He is on my side. Thank you, Father! I love you with all of my heart, mind, and will. In Jesus' name, I pray, amen.

**Prayer Confession Day 18: A Prayer of Confidence**

Lord, I boldly praise you for the infallible confidence you have given me. You are such a loving Father with great power and great plans for me! Thank you for reminding me nothing is impossible with you; nothing is too difficult for you to handle because there is no failure in you.

I confess you are my help and strength. Thank you for the mighty things you are doing before my eyes. I shall live and NOT die so that I may declare the marvelous works of my God! I confess I will behold and enter into everything you've called me to possess in this life. I have the victory! I believe it's already done, so I can confidently declare that I will demonstrate the tangible evidence of everything you have promised me, even as you are manifesting breakthrough for me!

I choose to reject every lie of the devil. Everything he has ever said to me is a lie. Thank you, Father, I am not a failure! It is impossible for me to fail because Jesus has already assured me victory. I will remain confident in you. Hallelujah! In Jesus' name, I pray, amen.

**Prayer Confession Day 19: A Prayer to Activate and Release Greatness**

Lord, thank you for reminding me today just how much greatness resides in me. I am your daughter. Since you are a great God, that means I have your DNA in me. Help me to recognize what is sometimes difficult to identify in myself although it is often easy to identify in others. Give me a greater resolve to fully embrace the greatness you've called me to live out.

Today, I acknowledge and accept every seed of greatness you have already deposited within me. I am a great person, just like my heavenly Father. I can do great exploits for your kingdom. I will not be intimidated by the magnitude of greatness you have called me to, but I will endeavor to approach it in humility and your grace.

I declare I can do all things through your strength and power. I declare that you make my feet like that of deer and have given me hinds feet for high places (Psalm 18:33). I declare I shall accomplish great exploits for you. I know you, I praise you, and I love you. In Jesus' name, I pray, amen.

## Prayer Confession Day 20: A Prayer of Courage

Dear Lord, thank you for giving me courage to wait in grace as I yet believe you to manifest every promise for healing and breakthrough in my life. I confess your courage to wait in peace and patience with great joy. I can confidently display courage to trust you as I wait because I know that everything has already been done!

I declare I have the courage to keep speaking life to my situation. I declare I have the courage to keep believing you for the fulfillment of every promise you've given me. I declare I have the courage to keep expecting the glory of God to be revealed on my behalf despite my present circumstances. I declare I have the courage to obey you even when it doesn't make sense to me or others. I declare I have the courage to stand strong in my relentless faith, anchored in your Word.

Just as you told Joshua multiple times to only be strong and very courageous, I too understand this is what I must do in order to access what you have already reserved for me. I boldly confess that I am possessing everything you've designated for me. There is no place for, and I refuse to give in to doubt, depression, disgust, discouragement, and disappointment. The warrior in me will stand up, every single time! Thank you, Lord, for how you have changed me through this process. I am graced to wait with great courage. In Jesus' name, I pray, amen.

**Prayer Confession Day 21: A Prayer of Praise**

Father, I praise you! You alone are worthy of my highest and best praise. When I consider who you are, and how you love me, I am completely overwhelmed! Your presence fills me completely. For this, I give you praise.

I know that everything that has been spoken from me to you, and you to me over the past twenty-one days has changed me for your glory. I am now in a place to receive what you have for me in a way I could not have fully embraced before. The journey has been for my good, and I am so grateful. I praise you for healing and breakthrough in every area of my life!

I am rooted in your Word, and I will never stop praising you for being my God, my Father, my Friend, and my Deliverer! You are always faithful to me! I am a warrior! Your daughter, but a warrior none the less. I win every time I worship! I slay every opposition every time I pray!

As I take the next ten days to deeply reflect upon and process all that has occurred over the past twenty-one days, I know you are going to continue to meet me at every turn and point. Thank you that I abide in you and you abide in me. I will never cease to rejoice in you and give you praise. In Jesus' name, I pray, amen.

# About the Author

Artist. Author. Ambassador. Those three words speak to the heart of Patrice Burrell.

She is passionate about all things worship! Rather it's singing about her love for God as a music recording artist, writing about it as a songwriter and blogger, or declaring the Word of God as a minister of the Gospel of Jesus, she loves pouring out her worship to God until it overflows to the hearts of others.

Patrice is called to exhort people that they might be edified and encouraged through the ministry God has entrusted to her. It is her privilege to share her passion for the glory of God, as she desires to see all God's people encounter His presence in their daily living.

The joyful mother of one daughter, Patrice and her family make their home in beautiful Orlando, Florida.

You may connect with Patrice on social media and learn more about Patrice Burrell Ministries by visiting her website:
www.patriceburrell.com

Printed in Dunstable, United Kingdom

66161093R00070